Liberalism:
*A Critique of Its Basic
Principles and Various Forms*

Liberalism

*A Critique of Its Basic
Principles and Various Forms*

(EXCERPT FROM THE *Tractatus
de Ecclesia Christi*, QUESTION XVII)

By His Eminence,
LOUIS CARDINAL BILLOT, S.J.

Originally translated by
Msgr. George Barry O'Toole, PH.D, S.T.D.

Revised English Translation and Introduction by
Thomas Storck, M.A.

Foreword by Fr. Thomas Crean, O.P.

*"Of old time thou hast broken my yoke,
thou hast burst my bands, and thou
saidst: I will not serve." Jer. II, 20.*

AROUCA
PRESS

Originally published by Archabbey Press, 1922
First translated by Msgr. George Barry O'Toole, PH.D, S.T.D.,
Professor of Dogmatic Theology,
St. Vincent Seminary, Beatty, PA
2019 © by Arouca Press
Foreword © Thomas Crean, O.P.
Introduction and Revised English Translation © Thomas Storck

*Citations from the original English work
have been incorporated as footnotes.
Editor's notes have been distinguished with a "†"*

ISBN 978-1-9991827-1-7

Arouca Press
PO Box 55003
Bridgeport PO
Waterloo, ON N2J3G0
Canada
www.aroucapress.com
Send inquiries to info@aroucapress.com

Cover and book design by
Michael Schrauzer

CONTENTS

FOREWORD

IT HAS OFTEN BEEN SAID THAT THE CATH-
olic Church's 'social teaching' is her best-kept secret. In fact, it
has been said so often that it seems that it can scarcely be true any
more, if ever it was. Yet the phrase is perhaps true as regards one part
of the Church's teaching on social matters: the duty of civil rulers to
put society beneath the reign of Jesus Christ. This social Kingship
of Christ, which constitutes Christendom, was lived before it was
systematically articulated. The emperor Theodosius I, the last man
to rule over the united Roman empire of East and West, commanded
that the Catholic religion be especially favoured in his domains. In
the following century, Pope Leo the Great, writing to his namesake in
Constantinople, Emperor Leo I, told him: "You ought unhesitatingly
to consider that the kingly power has been conferred on you not for
the governance of the world alone but more especially for the guard-
ianship of the Church" (Letter 156). The later struggles between the
papacy and the Western emperors over the right to appoint bishops
led to still stronger statements from popes and doctors about the
subordination of the temporal power to the spiritual one. Not that
the two powers were merged, as happens in Islam: the Catholic king
or senate was recognised as having their proper sphere, in which
they did not take instructions from the clergy. Yet the highest duty
of a temporal ruler was always so to govern that it might be easier
for his subjects to attain salvation, and if he stubbornly refused to
accomplish this duty, giving free rein instead to the enemies of the
Church, he might be declared deposed by the pope, to whom, as St
Thomas Aquinas writes, "all the kings of the Christian People are
to be subject as to our Lord Jesus Christ Himself" (*De Regno*, I.15).

The catastrophe of the French Revolution caused the popes to
express with ever greater clarity the duties of temporal rulers and

societies to God and to divine revelation. This process culminated in the establishment by Pope Pius XI in 1925 of the feast of Christ the King. Yet this liturgical proclamation of the right of the Word incarnate to reign over the temporal order was later described by the Scottish writer Hamish Fraser, Communist agitator turned ardent advocate of Christendom, as the greatest non-event of the 20th century. By this he meant that too many Catholic bishops had already made their peace with the Revolution, were embarrassed by the doctrine of Christ's social kingship, and desired nothing more than to be, according to the slogan popularised by the 19th century Count de Montalembert, "a free Church in a free State." Exactly forty years after the institution of the feast of Christ the King, at the 2nd Council of the Vatican, Pope Paul VI made Montalembert's aspiration his own, at least as far as practical politics went. The right of Jesus Christ to reign over the temporal order was not formally denied; but the doctrine was placed into a kind of suspended animation, and we still wait to see which pope will wake it from its sleep.

* * *

Louis Billot was one of the most theologically prominent champions of the principle of Christendom, in the early 20th century, and hence one of the keenest critics of the secularization of society by the Revolution. Born in France in 1846, he entered the Society of Jesus shortly after ordination. In 1885 he was made a professor of dogmatic theology at the Gregorian University in Rome, as part of the revival of the study of St Thomas Aquinas launched by Leo XIII with his encyclical of 1879, *Aeterni Patris*. Fr Gerald McCool SJ regards Billot as "the first really distinguished Neo-Scholastic theologian to be appointed to the Gregorian."[1] In 1909, Pope Pius X made him a consultor to the Holy Office, and, two years later, a

---

[1] G. McCool, *From Unity to Pluralism: The Internal Evolution of Thomism* (New York: Fordham University Press: 1989), 33.

cardinal. He wrote authoritative studies on a range of questions, including the two-volume treatise of ecclesiology, *De Ecclesia*, of which this present work is a short extract. Mgr Joseph Clifford Fenton would later write that Billot "will most certainly be counted among the very ablest of all the theologians who labored for the Church during the early part of this century."[2]

In some ways, Billot was not a typical theologian of his time. Independent minded, he tended to eschew the standard commentators on St Thomas Aquinas from Cardinal Cajetan onwards. Fr Romanus Cessario, in a recent lecture, noted that "those whom he [Billot] considers authoritative guides for doing theology inhabit mainly the thirteenth century; his list of approved authors comes to an end with Giles of Rome, who died in 1316."[3] A similar independence appears in the Jesuit cardinal's relations with Pius XI, pope from 1922. The pope had taken Billot's advice about the inadvisability of resuming the Vatican Council interrupted by the arrival of Italian troops in Rome in 1870; at the present juncture in Church history, the cardinal had presciently declared, a general council would give rise to discussions without end.[4] Later, however, when Pius XI condemned the French royalist movement, *Action Française,* Billot found it impossible to agree with the pope's decision, and became the only man in the 20th century to resign the cardinalatial dignity. Whether he jumped or was pushed is not clear.

It would be a serious mistake, however, to conflate the French cardinal's support for his country's monarchy and his opposition to its secularizing revolution. The kingship of Christ is not bound up with any one form of commonwealth, being able rather to

---

[2] Cf. J. Fenton, 'The Teaching authority of The Theological Manuals', *The American Ecclesiastical Review,* (Catholic University of America Press, 1963), 254–70. Fenton served as *peritus* to Cardinal Ottaviani during the 2nd Vatican Council.

[3] Published as 'Sacrifice, Social and Sacramental: The Witness of Louis Billot S.J.', *Nova et Vetera,* 14 (1), 2016, 131.

[4] B. Tissier de Mallerais, *Marcel Lefebvre: the Biography,* (Angelus Press, 2004).

accommodate monarchy, aristocracy, democracy, and any of the innumerable ways of mixing these three. If Billot opposed the French Revolution, it is principally on account of what he does not hesitate, in imitation of Joseph de Maistre, to call its "satanic" exaltation of liberty as the highest of all goods. To make such a principle the basis of society is, he points out, practical atheism.

Likewise, as the Jesuit author has no difficulty in showing, such a principle will in practice lead to the destruction of the most natural of societies, the family, and to the domination of atomized men and women by an "omnivorous" State. For the legislators of the Revolution, he writes, the family was in truth was the Carthage to be destroyed. While his imagination did not extend to the parodies of the family which have been installed by the legislators of our time, he would have recognised them as the logical outcome of what many of his fellow countrymen liked to call the "immortal principles of 1789." His prophecy of what the State becomes which denies its subjection to God and the Good is worth pondering:

> Over the scattered and disassociated monads which individualism has introduced, nothing can now remain except that gigantic and colossal State, an omnivorous thing, which, having destroyed all inferior autonomous organizations, will absorb into itself all force, all power, all right, all authority, and become the sole administrator, manager, instructor, preceptor, educator and guardian, until it becomes also the sole proprietor and possessor.

Billot has salutary words too for the one whom he calls the "Liberal Catholic," that is the man who wishes to marry the principles of the Revolution to the dogmas of the faith. If public authority treats the true religion as a merely human thing to which it need not subject itself, then not only does society as such sin against its divine author, but the true religion will also decay in men's souls:

Religion does not alter its nature when it passes from the public to the private order. If, therefore, in the public order it is reckoned among the merely human things which exist for a political end and are placed under the dominion of the State, likewise in the private order, by its very nature it takes its place as a mere human affair, for example, of an empty opinion concerning God, who, although in reality a sort of chimera, is still, nevertheless, thought to exist by superstitious and weak-minded men.

In other words, every State is a teacher: and if its laws and constitution teach atheism or agnosticism, even if only by their silence, most of the citizens will learn the lesson. Here Billot follows in the footsteps of his fellow countryman, Louis Veuillot (1813–83), whose book *L'illusion libérale*, sufficiently declares its thesis by its title; it is an illusion, these authors hold, to suppose that the Church will flourish more, the more it is divested of the favour of kings and parliaments. Nor, Billot insists, is it permissible to admit the principles of Christendom in the abstract, while holding that in practice the establishment of the true religion does more harm than good: "If *a priori* the principles express an order instituted and intended by God, it is impossible that their neglect should result in greater utility to the Church."

The reader may find Billot's style somewhat fierce and rhetorical. He is reminded that the author wrote in Latin, a language which among its other merits confers an elevation of tone that is lost in translation. This should not prevent any serious student from seeing the merits of this short work. Its central message? We must have either Christendom or tyranny.

Thomas Crean, O.P.

INTRODUCTION

CARDINAL BILLOT'S DISCUSSION OF LIB-
eralism, though contained in a book written in Latin a
hundred years ago, deserves to be much better known
than it is, for a grasp of the contents of this work will help the
reader to understand the society around him much better than a
perusal of political blogs or news sites will. Indeed, Billot explains
well much of the trajectory of American political and cultural
history, including much that has happened since the book was
written. For if Americans—by which I mean here, citizens of the
United States—wish to understand themselves and their country,
they must above all reckon with the meaning and significance of
liberalism. The term *liberalism*, however, is apt to be misleading,
and especially so for American readers, for in the United States
the term is used in a manner that is fairly unique in the world.
Therefore it behooves American readers to set aside their previous
understanding of the word and look at it afresh, as if they were
learning a new word in a foreign language.

What is liberalism, then, as used here? We may define it roughly
as that general movement in Western civilization which sought
freedom from the restraints imposed by Christian teaching, and
therefore has attacked Catholic culture initially on the political
and economic levels, then in the areas of marriage and sexuality,
and lastly, on the level of the human person itself. Or as Cardinal
Billot characterizes it, it is

> a many-sided doctrine which more or less emancipates
> man from God and from his law, from his revelation,
> and as a consequence frees civil society from all depen-
> dence on religious society, that is, from the Church

which is the custodian, interpreter and teacher of the divinely-revealed law.

We can see from this that liberalism champions freedom in the political and economic realms just as much as in the sphere of personal or sexual morality: liberalism promotes the free market as much as free thinking or free love. It is necessary to keep this in mind in order not to misunderstand the entire thrust of this book.[1]

As a Frenchman, Billot naturally makes much of the figure of Jean-Jacques Rousseau, who gave his own particular turn to liberalism, and who had a predominant influence in France. But the fundamental ideas upon which Rousseau based his political thought were in existence long before he published *The Social Contract* in 1762. They can be traced back to the corruption of the Aristotelian understanding of the formation of the body politic, and appear at least as early as Thomas Hobbes' *Leviathan* (1651), but assumed a shape that turned out to be much more influential in the work of another Englishman, John Locke (1632–1704).

What are those fundamental ideas? Cardinal Billot identifies the "fundamental principle of Liberalism" as placing

> the principal good of man in the absence of anything whatever that constrains or restricts his liberty, . . . hence, all those things which in any way limit or impede liberty are inimical and contrary to human perfection, and because, as is clear, many such fetters to this liberty arise from social relationships, therefore the ideal state of man is to be found only in an a-social condition, in

---

[1] Likewise, the reader should put aside the idea that there exist two mutually antagonistic blocs, liberals and conservatives, whose opinions and policies are at variance one with another. Such a binary way of understanding political philosophy distorts the variety and complexity of the political opinions and movements that exist and have existed.

which only the law of pure and perfect *individualism*
would reign supreme.

Here we already come to the heart of the matter. What is the
natural state of mankind? Aristotle had given an account of the
origin of society which proceeded from the family to the *polis*, the
former "established by nature for the supply of men's everyday
wants," which "when several families are united, and the association
aims at something more than the supply of daily needs," results in
the village. However,

> When several villages are united in a single complete
> community, large enough to be nearly or quite self-suf-
> ficing, the state comes into existence, originating in the
> bare needs of life, and continuing in existence for the
> sake of a good life. And therefore, if the earlier forms
> of society are natural, so is the state, for it is the end of
> them, and the nature of a thing is its end.[2]

The point here is that man's natural state is in community,
whether a family, a village or the final and most perfect form of
community, the *polis*. This understanding of man's natural condition became a commonplace of the Catholic tradition, and is
summed up by Pope Leo XIII in his encyclical, *Immortale Dei*
of 1885, in these words: "Man's natural instinct moves him to live
in civil society, for he cannot, if dwelling apart, provide himself
with the necessary requirements of life, nor procure the means of
developing his mental and moral faculties" (no. 3).
But there is a very important consequence which follows from
this, as Pope Leo went on to say, that

[2] Aristotle, *Politics*, I, 2 (Oxford translation).

as no society can hold together unless some one be over all, directing all to strive earnestly for the common good; every civilized community must have a ruling authority, and this authority, no less than society itself, has its source in nature, and has, consequently, God for its author. (no. 3)

It is obvious that if a ruling authority in society is as natural as society itself, then it cannot possibly be the case that that authority is any hindrance to or restriction on whatever are man's natural liberties. The natural state of humanity is not only in society, but in a society with a ruling authority, and thus it is perfectly in accord with human nature that society will place restraints upon human conduct, indeed, such restraints are necessary for the perfection of our nature.

In the early modern period, however, this understanding of the origin and nature of society began to be challenged. Although the Anglican theologian Richard Hooker, in his *Laws of Ecclesiastical Polity* (1593), continued substantially in the tradition of Aristotle and still taught that "we are not by ourselves sufficient to furnish ourselves with competent store of things needful for such a life as our nature doth desire, a life fit for the dignity of man," and that "societies could not be without Government,"[3] new notions were soon to arise. According to Thomas Hobbes, man's natural state is not in society, but is one of an a-social, even anti-social, freedom, in which there is no right nor wrong, a state of war in which "nothing can be unjust." Since "there is no common power" there is "no law," and "Naturally every man has right to every thing," and "every man is enemy to every man." It takes little reflection to realize how dangerous and unpleasant such an existence would be, and Hobbes himself sums up such a life in his famous phrase as "solitary, poor, nasty, brutish, and short."[4]

[3] Book I, X, [1].
[4] Thomas Hobbes, *Leviathan: or the Matter, Forme and Power of a Commonwealth Ecclesiastical and Civil.* Quotations from chapters 13 and 14.

Hobbes has little difficulty in arguing that from such a condition
men would be impelled to seek not only society, but an ordered
society for the sake of "their own preservation, and of a more con-
tented life [than] that miserable condition of war."[5] As a result,
mankind has instituted political societies or commonwealths by a
formal agreement with one another, or a *covenant*, as Hobbes calls
it. This covenant is what we are more accustomed to call the *social
contract*. But however understandable it is that people living under
the conditions of Hobbes' state of war would seek to end that state
by agreeing to enter into society, the crucial point is that, when all is
said and done, such a society is still not the natural state of mankind.
The restrictions imposed by such a society, even if entirely necessary
and understandable, are artificial and even unnatural restraints upon
our conduct and our original liberty. They "are contrary to our natural passions."[6] Since the state of nature for Hobbes is so disagree-
able, it is easy to avoid the logical consequences of this point. But
its importance will become clear as we look at the thought of Locke.

It is especially important for Americans to recognize the implications of John Locke's political thought. The historian Louis Hartz
wrote that in America Locke is a "massive national cliché" who
"dominates American political thought, as no thinker anywhere
dominates the political thought of a nation."[7] Since Locke's conception of the "state of nature" is couched in more positive terms than
that of Hobbes, this makes him the more appealing political thinker.
In his *Concerning Civil Government, Second Essay* he thoroughly
discusses this "state of nature" and man's reasons for leaving it.

To understand political power aright, and derive it from
its original, we must consider what estate all men are

[5] *Leviathan*, chap. 17.
[6] *Leviathan*, chap. 17.
[7] Louis Hartz, *The Liberal Tradition in America* (New York: Harcourt, Brace
& World, 1955), p. 140.

> naturally in, and that is, a state of perfect freedom to
> order their actions, and dispose of the possessions and
> persons as they think fit, within the bounds of the law
> of Nature, without asking leave or depending upon the
> will of any other man. (no. 4)

Immediately we see here a significant contrast with Hobbes. Instead of a situation in which since "there is no common power" there is "no law," for Locke mankind in this state was indeed subject to law.

> The state of Nature has a law of Nature to govern it,
> which obliges every one, and reason, which is that law,
> teaches all mankind who will but consult it, that being all
> equal and independent, no one ought to harm another
> in his life, health, liberty or possessions.... (No. 6)

But just as in Hobbes, if for less pressing motives, men are impelled to seek and eventually to enter into society. "God, having made man such a creature that, in His own judgment, it was not good for him to be alone, put him under strong obligations of necessity, convenience, and inclination, to drive him into society...." (no. 77). The first society was the family, but in time mankind sought to "join and unite into a community for their comfortable, safe, and peaceable living, one amongst another, in a secure enjoyment of their properties, and a greater security against any that are not of it" (no. 95).

It is important to note that, although Aristotle also recognized in the family the first kind of society, there is a crucial difference between his thought and that of Locke. For Aristotle the transition from the family to the village and finally to the full political community was a natural progression, not one that required at any point an explicit renunciation of man's natural freedom for the state of society. If man is a political animal, then it is just as proper to his nature, considered as a whole, to live in a political community as in a family. He is incomplete without it, and that community, although obviously made up of individuals, is more than simply a collection of individuals, but has in itself an essential function to pursue and realize the good, a function that no other entity has. As Josef Pieper wrote,

> The state, we may note, occupies a unique place in the scale that extends from the individual to the whole of mankind; more than anything else, it represents the "social whole." The idea of the common good is its distinctive attribute. A nation (in the midst of other nations) ordered in a state is the proper, historically concrete image of man's communal life. *Communitas politica est communitas principalissima* — Political community is community in the highest degree. In the fullest sense the state alone incorporates, realizes, and administers the *bonum commune*. That does not mean, however, that the family, the community, free associations, and the Church are not important for the realization of the common good, too. But it means that the harmonizing and integration of nearly all men's functions occurs only in the political community.[8]

The reader should keep in mind the contrast between Aristotle and Locke as we consider the influence that the latter's thought has had on American political and juridical thinking.

Although people enter into society because of disadvantages experienced outside it, in Locke's thought this entrance into society

---

[8] *The Four Cardinal Virtues* (Notre Dame: University of Notre Dame, 1966) p. 85.

cannot be regarded as lessening any of the real advantages that his understanding of man's natural state provided.

> But though men when they enter into society give up
> the equality, liberty, and executive power they had in
> the state of Nature into the hands of the society…, yet
> it being only with an intention in every one the better
> to preserve himself, his liberty and property (for no
> rational creature can be supposed to change his con-
> dition with an intention to be worse), the power of
> the society… can never be supposed to extend farther
> than the common good, but is obliged to secure every
> one's property by providing against those three defects
> above mentioned [the lack of a "known law" that reg-
> ulates conduct, of a "known and indifferent judge" of
> differences that arise, and the lack of sufficient power
> to punish evildoers] that made the state of Nature so
> unsafe and uneasy. (no. 131)

From this intention not to worsen his condition it follows that government exists only to secure or promote the chief goods that men already possessed in their pre-political state, their "liberty and property."

> The great and chief end, therefore, of men uniting into
> commonwealths, and putting themselves under govern-
> ment, is the preservation of their property; to which
> in the state of Nature there are many things wanting.
> (no. 124)[9]

---

[9] We may note here that Locke uses the term *property* as a shorthand for "lives, liberties and estates, which I call by the general name — property" (no. 123).

Cardinal Billot notes this same point as follows:

> Because if society is by no means natural to men, indeed
> if it is positively contrary to the intention of nature,
> accordingly and to the extent that it is opposed to
> the inalienable rights of liberty, then there is nothing
> whereby it can be in any way justified, unless it takes its
> origin from liberty, and is artificially constructed, pre-
> meditatedly and by express intention, for the supreme
> end of preserving liberty intact.

We find this Lockean idea expressed in the American Declaration
of Independence, namely that men "are endowed by their Creator
with certain unalienable Rights" and that "to secure these Rights,
Governments are instituted among Men." From this follows the further notion that the role of government is *negative*, limited to secur-
ing pre-existing rights which carry over from the state of nature,
and protecting their exercise against evildoers. The mainspring
and motive power of society cannot ever rest with the governing
authorities, but only in individuals. Hence the common reflexive
American idea that views government as more part a problem than
a solution, as something which should be limited or reduced as
much as possible, and whose regulations are more often than not
unnecessary or counterproductive.

Connected to the purely negative understanding of the role of
government is the notion that without human sin government or
civil society would not be necessary. As Locke says, "were it not
for the corruption and viciousness of degenerate men, there would
be no need" to form particular civil societies (no. 128). Or as James
Madison expressed it in *Federalist* no. 51, "If men were angels, no
government would be necessary." But as in the question of the natural state of man, here again Catholic tradition disagrees with Locke.
St. Thomas Aquinas teaches that even had mankind never sinned, a

kind of government would still be necessary,[10] a subjection proper to the free man, when someone directs him to his own good or to the common good. And the chief reason given by Aquinas for this is because man is "naturally a social animal" and "social life cannot exist unless someone presides who aims at the common good." So according to Aquinas, it is not "the corruption and viciousness of degenerate men" that makes civil society and social authority necessary, but the very nature of man.

This view of St. Thomas has been seconded by the popes themselves, who historically have made clear that the Church rejects the Lockean understanding of the state as being merely a negative power against sin or disorder. Pope Pius XI, for example, in his 1931 encyclical *Quadragesimo Anno*, discussing the earlier encyclical of Leo XIII, *Rerum Novarum*, rejects the view that governmental authority is limited to those matters only which are occasioned by human wickedness.

> With regard to the civil power, Leo XIII boldly passed beyond the restrictions imposed by liberalism, and fearlessly proclaimed the doctrine that the civil power is more than the mere guardian of law and order, and that it must strive with all zeal "to make sure that the laws and institutions, the general character and administration of the commonwealth, should be such as of themselves to realize public well-being and private prosperity." (no. 25)

In the view of Locke and Madison, however, since government has merely a negative role, it exists only because men are driven by passions, because they are apt to use force and fraud against their fellows. Moreover, the only positive force moving human society is the sum total of individual private choices and acts made by the

[10] *Summa Theologiae* I, q. 96, art. 4.

many individuals who make up society, each pursuing his own notion of happiness in his own way. Aristotle had noted that people differ radically in what they think is happiness,[11] but it follows from Locke's perspective that whatever subjective idea of happiness or the good an individual has, this is none of the government's business. So long as each individual's pursuit of what he regards as his good does not infringe upon his neighbor's natural rights, one ought generally to be free of governmental restraint. As a contemporary adherent of this view, Fr. Robert Sirico, put it: "So long as individuals avoid forceful or fraudulent actions in their dealings with one another, government is to stay out of their business."[12] To most Americans the logic of this assertion seems unassailable, for it is simply second nature to see the individualist viewpoint as obvious, while it requires an effort to understand the view that sees the governing authority as having, in Josef Pieper's words, the task of the "harmonizing and integration of nearly all men's functions."

The individualism which Locke promoted and which has been imbibed by so many Americans is perhaps most evident in the economic sphere of the United States, and, to a lesser extent, in other English-speaking countries. The 18th century deist notion of the economy as a self-regulating mechanism in which any, or almost any, attempt to regulate or adjust the economy from the outside on behalf of the common good constitutes unwarranted interference, fits very well with Locke's notion of man's natural state as outside of society and of the government as having no positive role. But in opposition to this Enlightenment viewpoint Cardinal Billot makes himself very clear. He explains the hostility of the liberal state to the family, and proceeds to explain that this hostility does not stop there, but extends to other subordinate societies, including corporations.[13]

---

[11] *Nicomachean Ethics*, I, 4.
[12] *Acton Notes*, vol. 8, no. 1, January 1998, p. 1.
[13] This term *corporation* is apt to be misunderstood by English-speaking

But do not imagine that other lesser societies can find favor in its eyes: such, for example, as those which were called *corporations*, like the guilds of artisans, of laborers, and in general, of men whom the exercise of the same art connaturally, as it were, associates together under fixed statutes and laws. The individualism of the social contract does not tolerate any such societies. . . . But the pretext was always the same: the liberty of the individual must be preserved intact, a free scope must be left for the competition of individual liberties, and that anything is contrary to the principle of liberty which either impedes or diminishes the free exchange of labor demanded and the wages offered. . . .

Billot quotes approvingly Charles Maurras' caustic comments on liberalism's attack on workers' right to organize — all in the name of individual freedom.

In the economic order, the principle of liberty wills that the sum total of the specific liberties, from which good ought inevitably result, should be a sacred arrangement. There is to be no other policy than *laisser faire* and *laisser passer*. The law of labor must apply only to the individual. [The] workman must . . . strictly forgo all association, guild or federation, every trade union, calculated to disturb the free play of supply and demand, the freedom of contract. So much the worse if the

---

readers. Corporation here does *not* mean a business corporation, a limited liability company, which is what it means generally in the English-speaking world, but an association of craftsmen or workers, such as the medieval guilds or a modern labor union. In Romance languages, corporations in the Anglophone sense are denoted by some version of the phrase *société anonyme* (French), *sociedad anónima* (Spanish), *società anonima* (Italian), and so forth.

contractor for labor is a millionaire, absolute master
of the fate of 10,000 workmen. Liberty! Liberty! Economic liberty, therefore, ends by a rapid deduction in
the famed liberty to die of starvation.... All real liberty,
all practical liberty, all free and assured power of preserving one's life, and of sustaining one's vital energies,
is denied the laborer inasmuch as one denies him the
freedom of association.

The attitude of liberalism toward religion looms large in Cardinal Billot's treatise, and here likewise the Lockean conception of
the state is implicated in the same fundamentally anti-religious attitude as the more explicitly anti-religious liberalism that the French
Revolution promoted.

The essential irreligiousness or impiousness of the principle of liberalism anyone will readily see who duly considers the fact that it was the cardinal principle of that
great *Revolution*, of which it has been said with truth that
it has a satanic character so explicit, so visible, that it is
distinguished thereby from every other event that was
ever seen throughout the whole previous course of history.

When we recall the attack on cloistered women religious, and the
martyrdoms of those whose only offense was that they wished to
remain in their congregations and serve God in silence and penance,
we can see that Billot hardly exaggerates when he terms this revolution
"satanic." Frequently writers will distinguish the liberal tradition as
it developed in England and Scotland and North America from the
continental tradition that gave birth to such horrible acts of violence
in 1789 and thereafter. Locke, it is held, was by no means hostile to
religion, and thus the regimes which were influenced by his thought
are likewise not enemies of religious faith, at least not historically.

But this is a misunderstanding. The logical implications of Locke's conception of society and the state are equally, though in a more subtle manner, destructive of religion as a real social and cultural force. Readers will recall the reasons Locke adduces for men forming a political community. "The great and chief end, therefore, of men uniting into commonwealths, and putting themselves under government, is the preservation of their property." As a consequence, as he states it in his (first) *Letter Concerning Toleration* of 1689, this commonwealth and its government exist only for the protection of those worldly goods which he calls "property" or "civil interests."

> The commonwealth seems to me to be a society of men constituted only for the procuring, preserving, and advancing their own civil interests.
>   Civil interests I call life, liberty, health, and indolency of body; and the possession of outward things, such as money, lands, houses, furniture, and the like.[14]

The state's duty, therefore, is "by the impartial execution of equal laws, to secure unto all the people . . . the just possession of these things belonging to this life" and "neither can nor ought in any manner to be extended to the salvation of souls. . . . "[15] Hence the state has no official opinion on any religious matters, and has no concern with morality beyond what is necessary for keeping public order.

Here we immediately see a major difference from the understanding of political society found in Catholic teaching and tradition. Thomas Aquinas in his *De Regimine Principum* writes, "It seems moreover to be the purpose of the multitude joined together to live according to virtue . . . the virtuous life therefore is the purpose of

---

[14] *Letter Concerning Toleration*, p. 3. All references to the *Letter* are to the edition published in the Encyclopaedia Britannica Great Books series (Chicago: Encyclopedia Britannica, c. 1952) vol. 35.
[15] *Letter*, p. 3.

the human community," and even adds that "the ultimate end of
the multitude joined together is not to live according to virtue, but
through virtuous living to attain to enjoyment of God,"[16] while in
the *Summa Theologiae* he states that "human law aims to lead men
to virtue. . . . "[17] But if men living in community aim at virtue, then
it follows that the community as such must in some way officially
acknowledge what is and is not virtuous.

Pope Leo XIII was even more explicit about the commonwealth's
relationship to things of a higher order than the "life, liberty, health,
and indolency of body; and the possession of outward things" of
the Lockean state. In *Immortale Dei*, he wrote,

> As a consequence, the State, constituted as it is, is clearly
> bound to act up to the manifold and weighty duties
> linking it to God, by the public profession of religion.
> Nature and reason, which command every individual
> devoutly to worship God in holiness, because we belong
> to Him and must return to Him, since from Him we
> came, bind also the civil community by a like law. For,
> men, living together in society are under the power of
> God no less than individuals are, and society, no less than
> individuals, owes gratitude to God who gave it being
> and maintains it and whose ever-bounteous goodness
> enriches it with countless blessings. Since, then, no one
> is allowed to be remiss in the service due to God, and
> since the chief duty of all men is to cling to religion in
> both its teaching and practice — not such religion as they
> may have a preference for, but the religion which God
> enjoins, and which certain and most clear marks show
> to be the only one true religion — it is a public crime

[16] I, 14. This work is also known as *De Regno*.
[17] I-II, q. 96, a. 2, ad 2.

to act as though there were no God . . . or out of many
forms of religion to adopt that one which chimes in with
the fancy; for we are bound absolutely to worship God
in that way which He has shown to be His will. (no. 6)

The Lockean state, however, is utterly indifferent to the question
of whether any religious truth exists and what it might be, and
hence, on a practical level, atheistic.

Another thing that follows from this deliberate exclusion of religion and morality from the state's purview is the appropriate level
at which discourse concerning the ultimate good for man ought to
take place. If the community as such is concerned only with external and this-worldly matters, then any opinions about religion or
morality are *ipso facto* merely private opinions, private concerns of
individuals, even if those individuals should happen to constitute
a majority of the population. The ruling authority as such has no
opinion and no concern in the matter. Each person's understanding
of the good is his own business, and although he is no doubt generally free to argue for his own conception of the good, regardless of
how many others he might convince to share his view, it remains a
private view. The political community's concern is necessarily limited to protection of rights and public order and it has no interest
in whether there is a supreme good for man that can be ascertained.
And since religion is not part of the serious business with which the
political authorities are occupied, it is hard to see why it should be
a part of the serious business of society either. The Lockean type of
government and the society which it fosters has no interest in the
truth or falsity of religious opinions, and judges all actions solely
on the basis of the secular criteria for which it came into existence.[18]

---

[18] Perhaps this is the reason why American Christians are usually more inter-
ested in moral than doctrinal questions, for the former often have implications for
our lives in this world, while the latter can seem merely "academic," not relevant
to our actual lives.

But as Cardinal Billot notes, when religious questions are relegated to the private order, they become "an empty opinion concerning God, who, although in reality a sort of chimera, is still, nevertheless, thought to exist by superstitious and weak-minded men." For if the community as such has no interest in religion, it is hard to see why any private person should. If religion cannot play any role in the political or public life of a nation, then why should it be important to the individual either, except perhaps as a psychological crutch or a merely subjective aid to personal rectitude for "superstitious and weak-minded men"? A God whom our rulers can officially ignore would hardly be a God that private citizens need worry much about. As we turn now to the question of religious liberty we will see more fully the implications of this view.

In his *Letter Concerning Toleration* Locke writes to promote harmony among various religious sects.

> The toleration of those that differ from others in matters
> of religion is so agreeable to the Gospel of Jesus Christ,
> and to the genuine reason of mankind, that it seems
> monstrous for men to be so blind as not to perceive the
> necessity and advantage of it in so clear a light.[19]

Thus a fellow citizen's religious opinions would have nothing to do with how well he will obey the laws of the commonwealth, and are of no concern to his neighbor.

> If a heathen doubt of both Testaments, he is not there-
> fore to be punished as a pernicious citizen. The power
> of the magistrate and the estates of the people may be
> equally secure whether any man believe these things or
> no.... [For] the business of laws is not to provide for

---

[19] *Letter*, p. 2.

the truth of opinions, but for the safety and security of
the commonwealth and of every particular man's goods
and person.[20]

Since the power of the civil authority extends only to material
things, it would appear that Locke has established a regime of the
utmost religious freedom, in which each and every person could
worship God or gods in any matter of his choosing. But Locke
has to deal with an obvious objection, that if absolute freedom of
religion is granted, what if some religion carries out outrageous
rites in its worship — "if some congregations should have a mind to
sacrifice infants, or . . . lustfully pollute themselves in promiscuous
uncleanness" — should this be permitted on the grounds that the
state may not meddle with spiritual matters? Locke answers: "No.
These things are not lawful in the ordinary course of life, nor in
any private house; and therefore neither are they so in the worship
of God, or in any religious meeting."[21]

This might seem a reasonable response, since, after all, could
anyone really expect that murder would be permitted under color
of religious worship? But Locke's answer not only rests upon the
state's indifference to religious truth, but also hides an ultimately
totalitarian view of the relations between state and religion, as we
can see if we look at another hypothetical example that he raises.

> [I]f any people congregated upon account of religion
> should be desirous to sacrifice a calf, I deny that they
> ought to be prohibited by a law. Meliboeus, whose calf
> it is, may lawfully kill his calf at home, and burn any
> part of it that he thinks fit. For no injury is thereby
> done to any one, no prejudice to another man's goods.

[20] *Letter*, p. 15.
[21] *Letter*, p. 12.

And for the same reason he may kill his calf also in a
religious meeting.

But he then adds,

> But if peradventure such were the state of things that
> the interest of the commonwealth required all slaughter
> of beasts should be forborne for some while, in order
> to the increasing of the stock of cattle that had been
> destroyed by some extraordinary murrain, who sees not
> that the magistrate, in such a case, may forbid all his
> subjects to kill any calves for any use whatsoever? Only
> it is to be observed that, in this case, the law is not made
> about a religious, but a political matter.... [22]

What is troubling about this? Note that the civil authorities
prohibit the killing of calves for a purely secular reason, because of
an outbreak of cattle disease. But if it were the case that God were
pleased or propitiated by the sacrifice of calves, would it not be the
case that that would override any purely secular reason? I am not
suggesting that the sacrifice of calves has any spiritual efficacy with
God, but simply pointing out that if the government is limited to
this-worldly considerations in its legislation and administration,
and can justly ignore religious considerations, this extends not only
to false religions but to the true religion as well. The fact that we
are permitted by Locke to believe whatever we like would seem to
have little meaning if our external acts are forced to conform to
standards determined solely by secular criteria. Thus it is society, as
much as the political order, that is rendered secular. The obvious
retort, that nations where John Locke has been a predominant
intellectual influence, such as the United States, are commonly

[22] *Letter*, pp. 12–13.

considered to be very religious, is neither here nor there. For potentially any and all of this religious activity could be stopped if the state declared it had a sufficient secular reason for doing so. In theory, all religious activity exists simply by virtue of the fact that it does not interfere with any important — and necessarily secular — state purpose.

If we briefly look at the religious liberty jurisprudence of the United States Supreme Court, we can see how this Lockean principle has been consistently applied. One of the clearest examples of this is the 1990 decision, written by Justice Antonin Scalia, in the case of Employment Division v. Smith.[23] In this case, two men, Alfred Smith and Galen Black,

> were fired from their jobs with a private drug rehabilitation organization because they ingested peyote for sacramental purposes at a ceremony of the Native American Church, of which both are members. When [Smith and Black] applied to [the Oregon] Employment Division . . . for unemployment compensation, they were determined to be ineligible for benefits because they had been discharged for work-related "misconduct."

On appeal from the Supreme Court of Oregon, the U.S. Supreme Court ruled against Smith and Black, because it determined that "neutral, generally applicable" laws which are directed to some secular purpose, and only incidentally infringe on religious practice, may be enforced even though religious believers are thereby inconvenienced. Oregon's law against peyote use was not directed against its sacramental use by the Native American Church, but was a general prohibition based on secular criteria. Justice Scalia wrote that, "We have never held that an individual's religious

---

[23] 494 U.S. 872.

beliefs excuse him from compliance with an otherwise valid law prohibiting conduct that the State is free to regulate." Moreover,

> the right of free exercise does not relieve an individual
> of the obligation to comply with a "valid and neutral
> law of general applicability on the ground that the law
> proscribes (or prescribes) conduct that his religion pre-
> scribes (or proscribes)."

The argument here is essentially the same as Locke's argument in the case of "some extraordinary murrain" that threatens a nation's stock of cattle. This conceals a latent totalitarianism because, under color of some "valid and neutral law of general applicability," the government may mandate or prohibit behavior that infringes upon religious belief. When there is an overwhelming consensus about what kinds of conduct are reasonable or customary, these totalitarian implications are not likely to come to the fore. Thus until recently, the traditional Protestant consensus that has governed American society has seldom been disturbed by disputes arising from the free exercise clause of the First Amendment,[24] and almost all the religious liberty cases that have been litigated in the United States have involved minority religions, whose adherents do things like marry more than one wife,[25] fail to salute the flag,[26] observe Saturday as their day of rest,[27] take peyote or sacrifice animals as

[24] This is the second clause of the First Amendment to the U.S. Constitution, "Congress shall make no law respecting an establishment of religion, *or prohibiting the free exercise thereof...* (emphasis mine).
[25] Reynolds v. United States, 98 U.S. 145 (1878), and subsequent cases. See note no. 33 for citations.
[26] The two flag salute cases were Minersville School District Board of Education v. Gobitis, 310 U.S. 586 (1940) and West Virginia State Board of Education v. Barnette, 319 U.S. 624 (1943). Both involved Jehovah's Witnesses.
[27] There have been several cases involving those who observe Saturday as the weekly holy day. They include Braunfeld v. Brown, 366 U.S. 599 (1961), which concerned Orthodox Jews, and Sherbert v. Verner, 374 U.S. 398 (1963), and Hobbie

part of a religious ceremony,[28] behaviors not part of the traditional conduct of most Americans. It is easy to see how one of these unusual practices might fall afoul of "generally applicable and otherwise valid" laws, even if the laws are not targeted specifically at religious conduct. For since general laws that deal with secular matters naturally reflect the way the majority of citizens live, or how they have traditionally lived, whenever minority religions depart from this way of life, there is a possibility that one of their religiously mandated norms of conduct will come into conflict with these laws. But it should be clear that this approach to the question subordinates potentially *all* religious conduct to policy decisions of legislatures and courts. For it is not difficult to imagine, given the right climate of opinion, a general law being passed prohibiting almost any form of religious conduct.

Two examples might suffice. About a hundred years ago the United States prohibited by constitutional amendment "the manufacture, sale, or transportation of intoxicating liquors."[29] Although the amendment and its enforcement legislation did not extend to the use of wine in Christian or Jewish religious rites, does it require much imagination to think that the society of that time might have deemed even religious use of wine contrary to a "compelling governmental interest," and thus outlawed Catholic, Eastern Orthodox, Episcopal and other religious rituals, as happened with peyote in the rites of the Native American Church?

---

v. Unemployment Appeals Commission of Florida, 480 U.S. 136 (1987), both of which concerned Seventh-Day Adventists.

[28] Church of Lukumi Babalu Aye v. City of Hialeah, 508 U.S. 520 (1993). This case involved adherents of the Santeria religion, which includes animal sacrifices in its rituals.

[29] Section 1 of the Eighteenth Amendment to the U.S. Constitution stated: "After one year from the ratification of this article the manufacture, sale, or transportation of intoxicating liquors within, the importation thereof into, or the exportation thereof from the United States and all territory subject to the jurisdiction thereof for beverage purposes is hereby prohibited." This amendment was ratified in 1919 and repealed in 1933 by the Twenty-First Amendment.

In this same era, immediately after World War I, occurred several attacks on the Catholic Church's right to maintain her own schools. Unsuccessful efforts were made in Nebraska, Michigan and Oklahoma, but in November 1922 Oregon by a popular referendum actually did enact a measure which "required all students from eight to sixteen to attend public schools."[30] In its defense of the law in the courts, Oregon argued on the basis of entirely secular criteria, asserting, as Locke had put it, that "the law is not made about a religious, but a political matter."

> Attorneys for the state argued that the "invidious poison" ruining the nation was "class hatred" that could be overcome by requiring "that the poor and the rich, the people of all classes and distinction and of all the different religious beliefs, shall meet in the common schools, which are the great American melting pot, there to become ... the typical American of the future."[31]

The decision of the United States Supreme Court, Pierce v. Society of Sisters,[32] which overturned Oregon's law, is often hailed as an outstanding instance of the triumph of religious freedom. But in the Smith opinion that I have already discussed, Justice Scalia asserted that the only reason the Pierce case was decided against Oregon was because the religious freedom claim was "in conjunction with other constitutional protections, such as ... the right of parents ... to direct the education of their children...." " It is true that the Supreme Court has often invalidated legislation held to

---

[30] Christopher J. Kauffman, *Faith and Fraternalism: The History of the Knights of Columbus, 1882–1982* (New York: Harper & Row, 1982), pp. 280–282. Quote from p. 282.
[31] David J. O'Brien, *Public Catholicism* (Maryknoll, NY: Orbis, 2d ed. 1996), p. 160.
[32] 268 U.S. 510 (1925).

violate the free exercise clause of the First Amendment, but when both the legislative and judicial branches share the same outlook, religious freedom claims can easily be overridden. In its campaign against the Mormons over the question of polygamy, Congress, the territorial legislatures and the Supreme Court went so far as to deprive polygamists or those supporting polygamy of the right to vote and hold public office, a prohibition later extended to any Mormon, and eventually in 1887 dissolved the legal corporation of the Mormon church and confiscated all its property, except for a portion actually used for religious worship.[33] Today such legislative and judicial actions are not likely to be used against those practicing plural marriage, but rather against individuals and religious bodies upholding the teaching of the natural law and Christian revelation on marriage and sexuality.

It is a paradox that the Lockean conception of the state both absolutizes individual liberty and conceals a totalitarian attitude toward religion. The reason for this is that society is seen as having no concern with anything except the goods of this world, and hence religious claims can be set aside when they are held to conflict with what are conceived to be freedoms and rights pertaining to this life. Hence the state, freed from any restraints imposed by God or the Church of God, need only consult the "civil interests" of its citizens. At the same time as it ignores its "manifold and weighty duties linking it to God, by the public profession of religion," and privatizes all concern for man's ultimate good, it turns around and asserts its right to regulate religious conduct according to secular or political criteria. Although the possibility of establishing a state that does live up to its "manifold and weighty duties linking it to God" is remote today, Catholics should resist the attempt to colonize our minds with social conceptions rooted in the alien tradition

---

[33] For the Supreme Court cases upholding these laws, see Murphy v. Ramsey, 114 U.S. 15, (1885); Davis v. Beason 133 U.S. 333 (1890); The Late Corporation of the Church of Jesus Christ of Latter-Day Saints v. United States, 136 U.S. 1 (1890).

of liberal thought. If we preserve our thinking free of distortions, then we will have done all that this generation seems to be asked to do. What tasks God will give those who come after us, he will show them in his own good time.

* * *

In revising Msgr. O'Toole's original translation I tried to balance three, sometimes conflicting, principles: Fidelity to the Latin, ease and naturalness of the translation for contemporary English-speakers, and disturbance of Msgr. O'Toole's original rendering as little as was necessary to achieve the first two goals. I hope I have not fallen short too egregiously in this, and I ask the reader's indulgence for any failures on my part.

Cardinal Billot included quite a few quotations from French authors in his treatise. These translations from the French are largely the work of my wife, Inez Fitzgerald Storck, and I am deeply grateful for her assistance in this.

Thomas Storck

August 21, 2019

PRELIMINARY NOTE

Concerning the Error of Liberalism and its Various Forms

L IBERALISM, ACCORDING AS IT CON-
cerns an error in the field of faith and religion, is a many-
sided doctrine which more or less emancipates man from
God and from his law, from his revelation, and as a consequence
frees civil society from all dependence on religious society, that is,
from the Church which is the custodian, interpreter and teacher
of the divinely-revealed law.

Liberalism, I repeat, which involves error in the field of faith and
religion. Because if you consider the meaning of the name, you will
easily perceive how liberalism thrives or is able to thrive not just
in those things which concern religion and our relations to God.
Indeed, emancipation from God was the end principally sought.
They came together against the Lord and against his Anointed saying, *Let us break their bonds and cast away their yoke from us* (Psalm
2). But for the sake of this end they maintained a general principle
that goes beyond the limits of the religious order, and pervades
and penetrates every part of human association. The principle is
this: Liberty is the fundamental human good, holy and inviolable,
which it is wicked to attack with force; and moreover, this same
unrestricted liberty ought to be put as the immovable rock upon
which all things in our human fellowship are *de facto* arranged, as
the immovable norm according to which all things are judged *de
jure*: so that, in the end, that condition of society is called equita-
ble and just and good which resembles this principle of inviolate
individual liberty; something that is otherwise, unjust and perverse.

This is what the champions of the memorable Revolution of 1789 came up with, whose bitter fruit is now harvested in nearly the entire world. This is what, in the Declaration of the Rights of Man, occupies the beginning, the middle and the end. This is what was the basis for those ideologies for the total rebuilding of society, in the political order, the economic, the domestic, and especially the moral and religious.

It is worthwhile therefore to describe in the first place the general crisis of liberalism, both in itself and according to its multiple applications in every sphere of affairs. From which then there will be an easier approach to a specific discussion of those matters which the present dispute concerns, namely, religious liberty and its various forms.

PART I

PRELIMINARY NOTE

Concerning the Fundamental Principle of Liberalism and its Manifold Applications

LIBERTY, AS IT CONCERNS US HERE, IS not precisely that which the metaphysicians discuss, namely, the power of free choice, consisting in the power which the human will has over its own acts, that is, in its ability to will or not to will, to will a particular thing or its opposite. For this kind of liberty, which is freedom from intrinsic necessity, which brings with it obligations of conscience, and which binds us to the observance of the moral law, liberalism is not at all concerned, and, so little does it care that many of its followers are absolute materialists, not recognizing in man anything beyond the principles of spontaneous movement according to instinct and natural necessity. At all events, whether they admit or do not admit free will, understood in its proper and metaphysical sense, they do not see in it the object of their idolatry, but rather in the power of exercising one's own activity, whatever that activity may be, without outside coercion limiting one's autonomy. This liberty, therefore, is freedom from all interference; and not only from coercion strictly speaking, such as by means of violence, but also from coercion through fear of the laws, by the threat of penalties, and through social pressures and ties, and, in a word, by bonds of any kind whatever whereby a man is prevented from acting, or being able to act, in all things according to his own individual inclination. Such liberty, they maintain, is the good *par excellence*, to which all else must yield, those things perhaps alone excepted, which are necessary for the purely material order of the commonwealth; a good so excellent that all other things must be subordinated in order to preserve it intact, and which necessarily must be the basis of all society, if the latter is to measure up to the true standard of goodness and equity. It will be well, therefore, to state in a few words what verdict must be passed upon this first principle of liberalism.

CHAPTER I

THESIS: *That the fundamental principle of Liberalism is inherently absurd, contrary to nature and chimerical.*

I T IS ABSURD I SAY, AT THE OUTSET, IN that it wishes to situate the principal good of man in the absence of anything whatever that constrains or restricts his liberty. For the good of man can be understood in only one of two ways, either as an end in itself, or as a means to an end. Now in which of these two categories, I ask, will you place liberty? Not in the former, I think. Because however you please to conceive the nature of an end, that at least without doubt you will grant me, that liberty cannot be an end in itself. For liberty signifies some sort of power or faculty of acting, and every power or faculty exists, not for its own sake but for the sake of something else, at least for the sake of its operation or action; which again, in this life, consists exclusively in the pursuit of some good, whether true or apparent. Very clearly, therefore, it must be said that liberty belongs to the class of goods which are means to an end, and therefore we can see that even common sense teaches us which goods are means to an end. Augustine distinguishes such goods into three categories, namely; the highest goods, the intermediary, and the lowest; and that for a very evident and obvious reason. He says that the supreme goods are those which no one abuses; the intermediary and lowest goods are those which admit of both a good and a bad use, with this difference only, that the intermediary goods are still required for a good life, while the lowest sort are in no way necessary for that. "The virtues, therefore," he says, "*by which* one lives rightly, are the

7

great goods; the types of corporeal things *without which* we *can* live rightly are the lowest kind of goods; the powers of the soul, without which one can*not* live rightly are the intermediate goods."[1] Now from this it is evident that free will can by no means be classified among the highest goods, but rather among the intermediate goods, because although there can be nothing praiseworthy or honorable in life without free will, neither is there any kind of crime or vice or harm to one's self or one's neighbor, into which it may not plunge head-long through bad use. Therefore liberty is in dire need of barriers lest it fall over the precipice, and, the stronger the restraints by which it is confined within the sphere of good for which it is ordered, so much the better is its condition. Whoever denies this by assenting to the fundamental principle of liberalism is compelled to choose between two equally absurd alternatives: either he will impudently affirm that liberty in the present life is incapable of misuse; or he will not fear to assert that it would be good, indeed best, if fallible liberty were to be sacredly and inviolably protected so as to facilitate even its *gravest abuses*. And what else is this than the greatest of insanity?

But these are merely the beginnings of insanity. A further step in that is what they add: everything is to be subordinated to the good of individual liberty; hence, all those things which in any way limit or impede individual liberty are inimical and contrary to human perfection; and because, as is clear, many such fetters to this liberty arise from social relationships, therefore the ideal state of man is to be found only in an a-*social* condition, in which only the law of pure and perfect *individualism* would reign supreme. And this, indeed, was the monstrous concept of the Revolution and its philosophers, who even, in order that they might seem to establish their abstract theories somehow or other, imagined the existence of a certain primitive condition in which man actually

[1] Augustine, *De Libro arbitrio*, 1. 2, C. 19.

lived outside society, adopting for this invention of theirs, the traditions of nations concerning a Golden Age, a Saturnian Reign, a
Paradise of Innocence, etc. For what, do you think, was that original
Golden Age? An age of absolute liberty, which gradually declined
into an age of iron, where more and more men came together into
society. Do you not see the principle of liberalism by its own nature
and unavoidable necessity ending in those things which are contrary
to nature? If there is anything evident, if there is anything manifest,
if there is anything clearer than the noon-day sun, surely it is that
man is born into society, that man is by nature social, that the social
state is for man the law of life, as even the necessity of his bodily
existence openly declares:

> For other animals nature has prepared food, garments of
> fur, means of defense, such as teeth, horns and hoofs, or
> at least swiftness in flight. Man, however, is constituted
> that, since he has none of these things prepared for him
> by nature, but in place of all these reason has been given
> him, by which through the work of his hands he is able to
> provide all these things for himself, for whose provision
> one man does not suffice. For one man by himself could
> not lead a sufficient life. It is therefore, natural to man to
> live in society. Moreover, in other animals there is inborn
> a natural instinct regarding those things which are useful
> or hurtful to them, as the sheep naturally knows the wolf
> to be its enemy. Some animals also by natural instinct
> are aware of certain medicinal herbs and of other things
> which necessary for their life. Man, however, has only a
> general knowledge of those things which are necessary
> for his life, being able to arrive by reason using univer-
> sal principles to the knowledge of the individual things
> which are necessary for human life. It is not, however,
> possible that one man gain the knowledge of all these

things by his own reason. Therefore it is necessary for man that he live in society, so that one can by helped by another and that different men, having discovered different things by reason, can be engaged one in medicine, another in this, another in that profession, etc.[2]

But none of these things deters dreaming sophists. For an immovable principle, which they do not even fear to derive from the law of nature, forbids this. For they think that they are uttering something great when they say: Man is born free; therefore anything that restricts this native liberty is contrary to nature. Just as if they were to say: Man is born naked, therefore it is contrary to nature that he is covered with clothes. But, though we are born naked, still we live clothed, and I think that the madness of insanity would not carry anyone to such a point that he would say that the perfection of nature has survived only in those tribes which in Oceania or Africa live just as they came forth from their mothers' womb. Moreover, what, may I ask, does this mean, that man is born free, except that he is born without impediments to the expansion of his own activity? And with similar liberty also, nature has endowed the animals as well as plants, so that for them, as was said above, from the moment they are born, nature provides garments and means of defense as well as other necessities. Hence, by virtue of their nature, from their very inception they shun what is contrary, and like what is beneficial, without any previous direction or instruction. Not so, however, the sons of men, not so. "Therefore, the Lord shows in this respect the lilies of the field and the birds of the air to be in a better condition than man, by comparing their need to that opulent King Solomon who enjoyed such exceptional abundance. *"Behold,"* he says, *"the birds of the air, for they do not sow, neither do they reap, nor gather into barns. Consider the lilies of*

---

[2] St. Thomas Aquinas, *De Regno*, Bk. 1, ch. 1, v. 6.

the field, how they do not labor, neither do they spin." Afterwards he
adds: *"I say to you, not even Solomon in all his glory was clothed as
one of these;"* as if Solomon stood in greater need in respect to food,
clothing and covering than the plants and animals."[3] And so it is
in truth. The brute animals would be in a better condition than
men, indeed, incomparably so, if once we were to suppose that man
is not a social or political animal by an institution of nature, and
that he ought not to be compensated by the benefit of society for
that which nature has denied to the individual. For the rest, are we
really serious or do we wish to jest? For that the liberty with which
men are born is nothing more nor less than the fullest liberty of
passing from the womb to the tomb, is perfectly plain and clear.
Insensate sophists, who has caused you to become so crazy so that
while continually appealing to nature, you commit so many and
such great outrages against nature?

But if the fundamental principle of liberalism begins with an
absurdity, and if from that it proceeds to those things which are
contrary to the clearest intention of nature, what now must be said
of the chimeras which it has laid down and defined in social matters,
after the likeness of a norm or directing idea? For willy-nilly, the
necessity of living in society is imperative, and whether that is for-
tunate or unfortunate, there is now no going back to that primitive
state in which man lived as a child of the forest. Hence it behooved
them to be solicitous for such a social structure as would leave
intact the palladium of liberty, and combine together two things,
which might perhaps have been considered incompatible, namely,
individualism and *the social organism.* Et hic opus, hic labor! But
nothing is hard for ideologues, nothing is hard for those who build
in the air. And lo, liberalism has ready at hand to show you a society
planned according to the rule of goodness and equity, and born of

---

[3] Tolomeo da Luca, Bk. 4, Ch. 2

† Only Bks 1 and 2 up to Chapter 4 have been attributed to St. Thomas
Aquinas; Tolomeo was the continuator of *De Regno.*

the *social contract*, as they call it. Because if society is by no means natural to men, indeed if it is positively contrary to the intention of nature, accordingly and to the extent that, it is opposed to the inalienable rights of liberty, then there is nothing whereby it can be in any way justified, unless it takes its origin from liberty, and is artificially constructed, premeditatedly and by express intention, for the supreme end of preserving liberty intact. Posit therefore, an initial pact whereby men agree freely among themselves about living together under a common government and a common law. Posit especially such conditions of the pact which correspond exactly to the end in view and to the will of the parties to the pact. Moreover, the will of those participating in the pact is not to renounce their liberty, but merely to join together their individual liberties, so that from all these joined together shall be had one total liberty. Liberty is what alone is sought, which alone is bestowed in common, because all things are from liberty, by liberty, and for liberty. Of no importance, then, socially speaking, can be those differences which differentiate one man from another, of no importance those natural and historical contingencies, of no importance the ties of family or those of nationality, of no importance the diversity of talents, of aptitudes, of education, of culture, of acquired rights, as they are called, or any other things of this kind. All these things are entirely extraneous to the matter of the social contract. It is only a matter of liberty, and nature has endowed each and every man with equal liberty. Hence each and every man must come into society on absolutely equal terms with his fellows. Count now the individuals, and that will exactly equal the number of votes: which, if they express a unanimous voice, nothing is better: if not, there remains the numerical majority (one-half plus one), which expresses the general will, and expressing the general will, it will express also the general liberty. This is the law of the community reduced to the rigorous principles of philosophy at last. And does it not seem admirable to you?

However, not perhaps so wonderful, that amid the glare of philosophical light you may not discern the full and perfect exemplar of a chimera. Two things especially belong to the notion of a chimerical system: That it should not agree with any real things, and that it is composed from those ideal elements which do not cohere for the purpose intended, but rather tend to its destruction and ruin. Moreover each of these things is easy to perceive in the system of liberalism.

In the first place the system certainly does not correspond to real men as they exist in flesh and bone. I pass over the point that no one, except a dreaming philosopher, ever thought of entering human society by means of a free pact or contract. I pass over the fact that the absolute necessity of society, a necessity prior to every possible use of liberty, will be obscure only to one who perhaps has fallen down from the clouds, and whom society has not received as a baby, nor nourished as a youth, nor whom, finally, during his lifetime, society has not given benefits of every kind and of the utmost necessity. What of the fact that the very defenders of the social contract themselves give testimony on this point to the truth? For how is the entrance into society free, if, as they themselves confess, there is now no way open of returning to the state of original liberty? But overlook, if you please, all these things. Take only the social element which is assumed as the basis of the system. This element is the individual man, stripped of all differences of place, time, lineage and nationality, of all ties religious, domestic, social, political, whether created or acknowledged as a consequence of his natural or historical evolution down to the present day. Such a one is a man who is neither modern nor ancient, neither Occidental nor Oriental, neither a father nor a son, neither a young man nor an old man: in a word, an abstract man always the same in all individuals, always equal, having neither more nor less the power of reasoning and of acting freely. But such a man is a mere abstraction; such a man is a logical entity; such a man has his place in the tree of Porphyry, but not in the sphere of realities. And if he has no place

in the sphere of realities, then neither will the chimerical system
which they have created for his use.

> Apply the "social contract," if it seems good to you, but
> do not apply it to any other men than those for whom
> it was made. These are abstract men who do not belong
> to any century or country, pure entities conjured up
> by the wand of metaphysics. In effect, they have been
> formed by expressly eliminating all the differences which
> distinguish one man from another, a Frenchman from a
> Papuan, a modern Englishman from a British contem-
> porary of Caesar, and only that element is considered
> which is common to all. There is left nothing but an
> exceedingly scanty residue, an extract extremely atten-
> uated, of human nature, that is to say, according to the
> definition of the time, a being who possesses the desire
> for happiness, and the faculty of reasoning, nothing more
> and nothing less. From this pattern are cut many millions
> of beings absolutely alike. Next, by a simplification quite
> as glaring as the first, they are supposed to be all inde-
> pendent, all equal, without a past, without kin, without
> commitments, without traditions, without customs, like
> so many arithmetical units, all separable, all equivalent,
> and one has to imagine them as assembled together for
> the first time, and dealing with one another for the first
> time. From the nature which is supposed to be theirs,
> and from the situation which has been created for them,
> there is no difficulty in deducing their interests, their will
> and their contract. But from the fact that the contract
> is suitable to them, it by no means follows that it would
> be suitable to others. On the contrary, it follows that it
> will be suitable to no others, and that the unsuitableness
> will be extreme should one attempt to impose it upon

a living people; because it will have as a yardstick the immensity of distance which separates a hollow abstraction, a philosophical phantom, an empty likeness without substance, from a real and complete man.[4]

The constitution of 1795, just like its predecessors, is made for *man* as such. But *man* does not exist at all in this world. I have seen in my life Frenchmen, Italians, Russians, etc., but as to *man*, I, for one, declare that I have never met him in all my life; if he exists he is to me utterly unknown.... But a constitution that is made for all nations, is not made for any nation; it is a pure abstraction, a scholastic work made to exercise the mind according to an idealistic hypothesis, and which must be addressed to *man*, in the imaginary regions which he inhabits.[5]

But the chimerical character of the system reveals itself still more in this, that while constructed for the express purpose of preserving liberty intact, in reality, it tends entirely to the destruction and ruin of liberty. This appears at once and very clearly with regard to minorities, which are surrendered to the tyrannical dictation of the prevailing number, without any defense, and without any possible recourse. And yet this kind of ideal society was supposed to be such as would gather into one the individual liberties, so that each individual by obeying the law, would obey his own will, represented in the law and by the law! Indeed, not only as regards minorities, but also as regards the very majorities themselves, this

[4] Hippolyte Adolphe Taine, *La Révolution,* Tom. I, 1. 2, c. 2.

† He was a French historian and philosopher and cited as one of the main figures of French Positivism. He criticized the French Revolution for creating conditions of more absolutism instead of the much-vaunted idea of "liberty".

[5] Joseph de Maistre, *Considérations sur la France,* c, 6.

† Maistre (1753–1821) became one of the leading counter-revolutionary figures in France during and after the events of the French Revolution.

same thing will appear at first glance. Because majorities, while they prevail as regards arithmetical quantity, do not excel commonly in reasoning, in wisdom, in independent judgment, nor, finally, in all those things which really constitute them as men in their own right. And if one is not a total stranger to human affairs, he will easily see that such multitudes, if perchance they are admitted to the making of law, are wont to be the prey of agitators, revolutionaries, powerful men, and, in a word, of the oligarchies which, born of individualism, subjugate those majorities and use them as the instruments of their domination to further their own private interests and their own personal ambition. Hence, from first to last, that boasted liberty is resolved by virtue of the system into the privilege of a few powerful men, while either open oppression or slavery veiled beneath the lying appearance of emancipation awaits all the others. Such, I say, is the conclusion which now suffices for a summary examination of the system. So that, however, on account of the gravity of the matter, this may become more manifest and evident, and that at the same time it may become more and more plain how pernicious, how noxious, how deadly is the fundamental principle of liberalism, even in respect to the simple purpose of civil life, it will be necessary to take up its particular applications. This indeed in the section which follows.

CHAPTER II

THESIS: *That the principle of Liberalism, in its application to human affairs, entails the tearing apart and dissolution of all social organs, introducing everywhere the struggle for life, instead of harmony for life, which alone is the law of life. And that it extinguishes all real liberties by constituting a despotic State, absolute, irresponsible, omnivorous, to whose will and omnipotence there is no limit.*

IN THE FIRST PLACE, ONE SHOULD NOTE that there is no question of a perfect and complete application of a chimerical and unnatural principle. You may expel nature with a fork, it will return; nor will it ever be in the power of dreaming philosophers to construct a real society in conformity with their ideas, in the way that a potter has power to fashion the clay, to make at will any kind of pottery from one mass of material. For as evil, if it were whole and perfect, would not even be able to sustain itself, but would destroy itself; so also every system that is contrary to nature is in its fullness unsustainable, and thus cannot be implemented without meeting causes or agencies of many kinds which obstruct it, and react against it, and in part cancel the pernicious force of its principles. Thus the noxiousness of liberalism must not be judged solely from the effects which we see thus far actually realized. But it must be seen what the application of the system necessarily implies, also what evil it has in fact introduced in proportion to its actual influence, that is, considering the greater or lesser latitude allowed it by the greater or lesser resistance, either of religious faith, or of natural righteousness, or even of the simple instinct of self-preservation, according to the different circumstances of places and persons.

Having made this preliminary observation, as it is only right to do, in the first place consider now how the application of the fundamental principle of liberalism brings about of its own nature the destruction of every lesser society, natural or connatural, which, existing within the domain of the State, is distinct from the State or at least does not receive its charter from the State. This, indeed, becomes most evident *a priori* from what has been said, and it becomes still more manifest *a posteriori*, if you consult the legislation which has arisen from liberalism, that is, from the principles of the French Revolution.

In the first place, I say, it is made evident from what has already been said. For liberalism, for all that it is worth, intends the emancipation of the individual, for whom it maintains intact that supreme and principal good of man which is liberty. Moreover, it holds that society is repugnant to the emancipation of the individual, that is, organized society, society formed with stable ties and laws, society, in short, which truly deserves the name society — that one society and it alone excepted, which has been constituted according to the norm of the principles of the *social contract*. Again, only that society is the society of the *social contract*, which gathers together individuals like so many arithmetical units entirely equal among themselves, and in every way independent of one another, under one common government emanating from the sum-total of the individual wills, which society they call by the name of State. The consequence, therefore, is that liberalism is doomed, either to repudiate itself, or to proceed towards the dissolution of every society distinct from the State, not ever stopping in its unspeakable work of destruction or pulverization, until it reigns over perfectly disunited monads which are merely piled up as grains of wheat are piled up in a heap. This surely is what the principles of the system lead to with inescapable logic. But how they have been brought from the order of ideas into the order of facts, and how this is still happening today, is worth the effort to set forth briefly.

The first society of all has been instituted by God himself, the Author of nature, a society which is beneficent among all, anterior to all political society, responding to the more intimate affections of the human heart, and the more evident needs of both our moral and our physical life; I mean domestic society or the family. It itself will then, first of all, experience the adverse blows of liberalism, which, as much as possible, by every means and device, by every effort, by every resource at its disposal, intends the destruction and elimination of the family, so that you may rightly say that, for the legislators of the Revolution, this in truth was the Carthage to be destroyed. And it destroys it first in its foundation. For the foundation of the family is marriage, and indissoluble marriage, through an indivisible obligation binding both the man and the woman until the very end. Moreover, how contrary such an obligation is to the liberty and emancipation of the individual, everyone will see at first glance. Nevertheless, certain prejudices still continue to be rooted in the minds of men, which do not allow the intended reformation to be carried out hastily. And so it will begin with the reduction of marriage to the status of a mere civil contract, sanctioned only by the civil law. Then, from civil marriage it will be a mere step to legal divorce, and not without reason, because whatever may be bound by the authority of the civil law can also be dissolved and rescinded by the authority of that same law. Finally, from legal divorce a gradual and imperceptible descent will be prepared to a vague concubinage in which is to be found the most complete application of the principles of liberalism, and with this, no more vestige of the family will remain than exists among the brute beasts. You see, then, how liberalism intends by every means and device to accomplish the destruction of the family in its primary foundation. It likewise intends to destroy it in its authority. In the first place, it does so by means of laws depriving the father of the family of the power of free disposal of his property, so that it is now not lawful for him to give one of his children a greater portion than another, nor even to disinherit an unworthy offspring. But, secondly and especially, this is done through laws requiring public and compulsory education, whereby the education of the children is virtually taken away from the parents, and the entire control of the public school system given over to the civil authority in such a way that no right of intervening is authorized for any other authority whatever in respect to the discipline or course of studies, or concerning the choice or approval of teachers. And what remnant, I ask, will be left of paternal authority, when such legislation, reaching the ultimate end of its evolution, shall put into complete execution those things which until now it has merely desired? But if the family still happens to withstand so many and such great forces of dissolution, finally consider the laws of succession, which prescribe that on the death of the father or mother the property shall be equally divided, and that each of the children shall go his own way taking with him a portion of the scattered patrimony. Hence the family has now become a merely temporary association which death speedily dissolves and disperses to the four winds; with the stability of the family estate the continuity of the family down through the ages perishes; the perpetuity of its examples and traditions is abolished, and only individuals remain who pass away and vanish, one after another.

In this way, then, does liberalism aim with singular and furious effort at the destruction of the family, and for no other reason except that it sees in the family, thanks to the solidity of that institution as well as the efficacy of its influence, the most powerful resistant to its own nefarious purposes. But do not imagine that other lesser societies can find favor in its eyes: such, for example, as those which were called *corporations*, like the guilds of artisans, of laborers, and, in general, of men whom the exercise of the same art connaturally, as it were, associates together under fixed statutes and laws. The individualism of the social contract does not tolerate any such societies. But since they were easy to destroy, for that reason, the Revolution at its very inception chose by a single decree, by a single law, by a single intimation of its despotic will, to abolish them forever. And the pretext was always the same: the liberty of the individual must be preserved intact; a free scope must be left for the competition of individual liberties; and that anything is contrary to the principle of liberty which either impedes or diminishes the free exchange of the labor demanded and the wages offered, etc., etc. In vain will wise economists protest that which even ordinary common-sense at once says: that such individual liberty, without any protection of united effort, is altogether helpless; that this is not liberty by which the worker is able to labor, to acquire and to profit *as he wishes*, but only *as he can*, nor even according to a humane and just law of organized labor, but according to a mechanical and fatal law of unbridled and destructive competition; that the case of the man who sells his labor is not the same as that of the man whom conditions of labor force to accept a certain wage, because the employer of labor can choose among many men who are forced under the stress of dire necessity to consent to a wage more and more insufficient; this liberty, therefore, on the part of the worker, soon ends in the liberty to die of starvation, it is a negative liberty, an abstract liberty, a liberty altogether empty; from this liberty arises the inhuman struggle for life and that mighty curse of the modern age, proletarianism, that is, of the numerous class entirely deprived of all stable property, and reduced to a miserable condition of hereditary want, etc. "The proletariat, that is to say, the condition of the family detached from all property, appeared (under Revolutionary law) as a normal thing, instead of a social monstrosity."[1] "The existence of a numerous class destitute of all property, and living, as it were, in a state of hereditary privation, is a new and unexpected fact."[2] In vain, I say, will you, or anyone else of good

---

[1] François-René de La Tour du Pin Chambly, *Vers un ordre social chrétien.*

† La Tour du Pin (1834–1924) was a French politician and advocate of social reforms in the light of Catholic teachings.

[2] Pierre Guillaume Frédéric Le Play, *La Réforme Sociale, t. 1.*

and sound judgement oppose these and other similar things. For to what purpose do you appeal to equity? To what purpose to the rights of a just and beneficent liberty? These are beside the point. Liberty is not sought with the distinction of whether it is just or not just, beneficent or not beneficent. Liberty is sought for its own sake, liberty as such, liberty as an abstract idea. And this ideal liberty does not concede the right of citizenship except to individual persons, which, lest they offer any kind of restraint to each other, it wishes them to be devoid of all solidarity among themselves.

It is clear, then, that it is the task of liberalism to dissolve all the social organs into one. For, as the organs of the physical body are not molecules, or atoms, but rather limbs and members, so also the organs of the social body are not individuals, but the family, the guild and the municipality. And if once we suppose that their own proper structures are destroyed, it follows that all real liberties must perish utterly. And the reason is evident, because over the scattered and disassociated monads which individualism has introduced, nothing can now remain except that gigantic and colossal State, an omnivorous thing, which, having destroyed all inferior autonomous organizations, will absorb into itself all force, all power, all right, all authority, and become the sole administrator, manager, instructor, preceptor, educator and guardian, until it becomes also the sole proprietor and possessor. And what else, I ask, does this bring about except a monstrous servitude? The Apostle says that the heir, as long as he is a child, differs in nothing from a slave, because he is under tutors and guardians until the time appointed by the father. But something worse happens to that ward of the social contract. For that ward is not an immature young person, but a people of mature age; that people is not placed for a time in that condition in which it does not differ from a slave, but indefinitely

---

† Le Play (1806–1893) was a mining engineer and sociologist who later in his life came to appreciate more the role of the Catholic Church in the stability of society.

and forever; that ward is not under a tutor selected by the father, but under a master to whose will and domination there is, so far as the system itself concerned, absolutely no limit. Indeed, in its final analysis, the liberalism of the Revolution is resolved into that proposition which is condemned in the Syllabus of Errors, no. 39: "The state, as the source and fount of all rights, possesses a certain right circumscribed by no limits."

> In the political order, liberalism declares at the beginning of the *Contrat Social*, and in the first article of the *Declaration of the Rights of Man*, that man is born free. Liberalism would detach the individual human being from his antecedents, whether natural or historical. It would liberate him from family-ties, occupational ties and all other ties, whether social or traditional. Only because it is necessary to live in society and because society requires a government, will liberalism establish a government for society upon the basis of one man, one vote and majority rule. The majority, expressing what Rousseau calls the *general will*, for that reason will also, in a sense, embody general liberty. The will of the majority becomes from then on a decree of law against which no one or anything could have recourse, however useful and reasonable and however precious or sacred that person or thing may be. The principle of liberty establishes a rule which methodically ignores all individual forces and liberties. It boasts that it alone created the liberty of each individual; but in practice, history shows clearly that this individualism weakens individuals. This is the first effect. Its second is to tyrannize, without staying within the law, all individuals not belonging to the party of the majority, and thus to destroy the last refuges of real liberties.

In the economic order, the principle of liberty wills
that the sum total of the specific liberties, from which
good ought inevitably result, should be a sacred arrangement. There is to be no other policy than *laisser faire*
and *laisser passer*. The law of labor must apply only
to the individual. As much out of regard for his own
liberty, as out of veneration for the machinery of the
world, the workman must respect the injunctions of the
Chapelier law†, and strictly forgo all association, guild,
or federation, every trade union, calculated to disturb
the free play of supply and demand, the freedom of
contract. So much the worse if the contractor for labor
is a millionaire, absolute master of the fate of 10,000
workmen: Liberty! Liberty! Economic liberty, therefore,
ends by a rapid deduction in the famed liberty to die
of starvation. I should make bold to call it a negative
liberty, an abstract liberty, better still, a vanished liberty.
All real liberty, all practical liberty, all free and assured
power of preserving one's life, and of sustaining one's
vital energies, is denied the laborer inasmuch as one
denies him the freedom of association. It required the
decline of liberal ideas to obtain, in the economic order,
a certain degree of freedom of association. To extend
this liberty, to develop and nourish it, we must oblit-
erate every trace of liberalism that still exists in human
minds.... We must either exclude all liberalism, or else
forego all actual liberty.[3] ††

---

† Legislation passed on June 14, 1791 by the National Assembly during the
first part of the French Revolution banning guilds.

[3] Charles Maurras, *Libéralisme et Liberté.*

†† Maurras (1868–1952) was the founder of *Action Française* which was condemned by Pope Pius XI but later rehabilitated by Pius XII.

But, what sort of enigma, then, is this that a social system erected upon liberty, to liberty, and for liberty should lead *so evidently* to despotism and the elimination of all real liberty? And what new kind of marvel is this, that a political doctrine founded, as they claim, upon pure philosophy, should recognize the dictatorship of mere numbers as the supreme authority, than which there is nothing more anti-philosophical?

> It is necessary to exclude the principle of government by number, because it is absurd in its origins, incompetent in its exercise, pernicious in its effects.... We have too much respect for the people to say to them: It suffices to count the votes of the incompetent, in order to resolve questions of very general interest which demand long years of study, of experience or reflection. It suffices to collect and tabulate votes to resolve the most sensitive issues.... Government by number tends to the disorganization of the country. It of necessity destroys all that which moderates or tempers it, all that which differs from it: religion, family, traditions, classes, organizations of any kind, etc.[4]

And do you imagine that if there was only question here of civil liberty or of platonic philosophy, that such a doctrine or system would ever have reached so lofty a pinnacle of success? But, indeed, the real grounds were something else, and this something else continues to be the real grounds down to this very moment. What that something else is, now must be explained.

[4] Maurras, *Ibid.*, p. 9

CHAPTER III

THESIS: *That the principle of liberalism is essentially anti-religious, raising the standard of independence directly against God. And as a matter of fact whatever it has attempted under the false pretext of liberty, whether in the political or in the economic or in the domestic order are directed toward the purpose of eradicating from the world the worship of God, the religion of God, the law of God, indeed the very notion of God.*

THE ESSENTIAL IRRELIGIOUSNESS OR impiousness of the principle of liberalism anyone will readily see who duly considers the fact that it was the cardinal principle of that great *Revolution*, of which it has been said with truth that it has a satanic character so explicit, so visible, that it is distinguished thereby from every other event that was ever seen throughout the whole previous course of history.

> The French Revolution is unlike anything that was witnessed in past pages. It is *satanic* in its essence. (De Maistre, *du Pape, discours préliminaire.*)
>
> There is in the French Revolution a satanic character which distinguishes it from everything that was ever seen and, perhaps, from anything that ever will be seen. (Ibid., *Considérations sur la France*, c. 5.)

Now, impiety has never been absent from the world, and impiety has always been a crime; but it had never existed before with the same characteristic trait, with the same intensity and, particularly, with the same organization. Among the ancients generally, impiety proceeds in a rather peaceable manner: it expounds, to be sure; it disputes, it cavils, it ridicules; but it is devoid of acrimony. Lucretius himself scarcely yields to taunts and blasphemy, even when he traduces religion and denounces it as the fruitful source of evils. There was not then, to be sure, a religion which served to excite the anger and the fury of contemporary unbelief. When, however, the Gospel began to be preached, the fight against religion also began to grow stronger. Yet still there was moderation and measure, for the pagan persecutors, in order not to fight under the standard of irreligion, attacked the Christians as atheists and subverters of the ancestral religion. Then in the following centuries, if any standard bearers of impiety appear, they are very rare and isolated, not united together in a league, not especially agitated with the fury which we witness. Hence, even the man who may be considered the father of modern unbelief, Pierre Bayle,[†] in the very worst passages of his works, still differs considerably from his successors, so little inflamed does he seem with the desire of persuading and of making converts: doubting more than denying, arguing for as well as against, abstaining from the tone of bitterness, as though a stranger to the zeal of partisans. But finally, in the eighteenth century impiety grew into a true and formidable power. Then was for the first time revealed to our times the real character of impiety, the fury of impiety, and, if one may say, distilled into the pure juice of impiety. No longer the cold indifference of skepticism, nor the unperturbed irony of the infidel against anodyne errors, but implacable hatred, flaming anger and rabid frenzy. They attack religion as their principal enemy, and those who go by the name of *philosophers* go from a hatred of Christianity into a personal hatred of its divine author. In fact, by a kind of malice which would seem to be beyond human nature,

---

† Pierre Bayle (1647–1706) was a French philosopher and historian; although traditionally known as a skeptic philosopher, his philosophy has been difficult to describe since he was an anti-systematic thinker.

they place the very person of Jesus Christ in exactly the same place that a personal living enemy would be placed. Then, also, after entering into a covenant, with united force they swear to extirpate the *infamous one* from the world; they swear to eradicate it from earth, so that its name may no longer be remembered. Then they rise up against God directly saying: *"Depart from us: we do not desire the knowledge of thy ways, and who is the Omnipotent that we should serve him?"* (*Job* 21:14.) But now we must consider what for a long time had been the state of things in Europe. Religion, of course, had permeated intimately the entire social body from the bottom of the feet to the top of the head. For since with us all civilization took its origin from Christianity, and the ministers of religion had obtained everywhere a conspicuous and lofty pre-eminence in the political state, from this it had come to pass that everywhere also civil institutions and religious ones had become marvelously interwoven. For of all the states of Europe it could be said with more or less truth what an English historian said concerning the kingdom of France: this kingdom was constructed by the bishops as the hive is constructed by the bees. Now, therefore, the reason is manifest why among the impious promoters of the Revolution an anti-religious madness carries with it as a necessary consequence a hatred for social institutions, insofar as they were unable to be separated from the religious principle. The ancient structure for whose construction both nature and religion, united in a friendly compact, had labored incessantly was extremely dis-pleasing to them. Hence they decreed that it must be leveled to the ground and utterly demolished, to make room for a new social and political order which would be suited to the prime and principal goal of destroying all religion.

> It was not until the first part of the eighteenth century that infidelity became a real power. Thereupon it is seen to spread with incredible rapidity to every quarter.

From the palace to the cabin, it insinuates itself everywhere, it infests everything; it has invisible channels, an action secret but infallible, such that the most attentive observer, witnessing the effect, is sometimes at a loss to discover the means. Through an inconceivable prestige it manages to make itself beloved by the very ones of whom it is the deadly enemy, and the very authority which it is about to immolate stupidly embraces it just prior to receiving the blow. Soon a simple system becomes a formal association, which by a rapid transition changes itself into a plot, and finally into a grand conspiracy which covers the whole of Europe.

Then is manifested for the first time kind of impiety which belongs to no other than the eighteenth century. It is no longer the cold tone of indifference, or the malignant irony of skepticism, it is deadly hatred, the tone of anger, and often of rage. The writers of this epoch, at least the most noted of their number, no longer treat Christianity as a human error of no consequence, they pursue it as their chief enemy, they attack it with a vengeance; it is a duel to the death, and what would appear incredible did we not have the sad proof before our very eyes, is that some of those men who give themselves the title of *philosophers* advance from the hatred of Christianity to an actually personal hatred for its Divine Author. They hate him as one can hate a living enemy....

Nevertheless, since the whole of Europe was civilized by Christianity, and the ministers of religion had attained to great political standing in every country, the civil and religious institutions became commingled and, as it were, amalgamated in a surprising manner; so that it could be said of all the states of Europe, with more or less truth, what Gibbon has said of France, *that this kingdom was made by the bishops.* It was inevitable, therefore, that the philosophy of the century would not be slow to hate the social institutions, from which it was impossible to separate the religious principle. This is what happened; all the governments, all the institutions of Europe displeased it, because they are Christian and in the measure that they are Christian; a malaise of opinion, a universal discontent takes possession of all minds. In France, especially, the philosophical fury knew no bounds, and soon one single formidable voice, formed by the coalescence of so many voices makes itself heard crying out (to God) in the midst of sinful Europe:

Leave us! Must we forever tremble before priests, and receive from them the instruction it pleases them to give us? Throughout Europe truth is concealed by the smoke of the censer; it is time for her to come forth from the fatal cloud. We will no longer speak of you to our children; it is for them, when they become men, to learn if you exist, and what you demand of them. All that exists displeases us because your name is written upon all exists. We wish to destroy everything and to remake all without you. Depart from our assemblies, depart from our academies, depart from our homes; reason suffices for us. Leave us! [1]

Now, the pretext for introducing this new social order was liberty; its constitution, the social contract; the means, demagogy; the ultimate motive, however, the construction of the *atheistic* and *colossal* State, as the supreme arbiter of all rights, the omnipotent dictator of all that is licit or illicit, permitted or prohibited, under

---

[1] Maistre, *Essai sur le principe générateur des constitutions politique,* n. 63–66.

which the infamous name and worship of God were to be abolished forever. Toward this everything is aimed, to this end everything else is ordained as a means; to this end the destruction of the family, to this end the destruction of the guilds, to this end the destruction of the liberties both of communities and of provinces, so that in the end there may be nothing left but the power of the State, without whose authorization no one can move hand or foot throughout the entire universe. This is the end intended, not civil liberty. Liberty is the pretext, liberty is the idol to seduce peoples; the idol which has hands and does not feel, which has feet and does not walk; an inanimate god behind which Satan prepares to reduce the nations to a servitude far worse than that in which he bound the ancient world by means of the material idols of paganism. For the rest, that which is really at issue is nothing else than religion. "We wish to organize a humanity which can do without God" (Jules Ferry).[†] And again: Clemenceau: "Since the Revolution, we have been in rebellion against divine and human authority with which we, at one blow, settled a terrible account, the twenty-first of January, 1793."[††]

For the rest, if anyone wishes to be informed concerning the satanic spirit of the Revolution, from irrefutable and authoritative documents, let him consult the four volumes of Abbé Barruel, *Memoires pour servir a l'histoire du Jacobinisme.*

And again:

> There are many who speak and write of the civilizational
> struggle, but few who understand that this struggle is
> against the last and desperate attempt to extinguish the
> Christian ideal, and that modern civilization is prepared

[†] Jules François Camille Ferry (1832–1893) was a French statesman and one-time prime minister of France. He advocated the laicization of the State especially in education and an expansion of colonialism.

[††] Joseph Clemenceau (1770–1819) who wrote a history of the War in the Vendee against the revolutionaries.

to resort to any means whatever, rather than yield with regard to those things which it has obtained with such great labor. For modern civilization and Christianity are in contradiction, and therefore one must necessarily give place to the other. Modern progress can acknowledge no God save one immanent in the world, opposed to the transcendental God of Christian revelation, nor another morality save only that true kind, whose source is the human will determining itself by itself, a law existing unto itself. [2]

This, then, is the final conclusion of the present chapter: Liberalism seeks the overthrow of religion, when under the lying name of liberty, it enters the domestic, or the economic or the political order. But its description is not yet complete. It remains to say something concerning its various forms in relation to religion. For it does not keep to one method, but knows how to temper the rigor of its demands in the presence of those whom the portent of its impiety might still offend; indeed, it knows how to transfigure itself into an angel of light, and under an appearance of an empty good to ensnare the uncautious with certain sophisms. Therefore, we must now explain, in a few words, into how many kinds it is, as it were, divided.

---

[2] Karl Robert Eduard von Hartmann, *Religion de l'avenir.*

† Hartmann (1842–1906) was a German philosopher whose work, *The Philosophy of the Unconscious,* made him renowned.

PART II

PRELIMINARY NOTE

On the Various Forms of Liberalism in Religious Matters

THERE ARE THREE PRINCIPAL FORMS OF religious liberalism. There is *absolute liberalism*; there is *moderate* liberalism; and, finally, there is a liberalism to which it is difficult to give a name, because, since it involves a complete incoherence, it avoids every definition: this is proper to those who assume the name of *liberal Catholics*. Common to all three forms is to promote the emancipation of the civil order from the religious, and thereby of the State from the Church. But in the first form this emancipation is brought about by means of the absolute domination of the State over the Church. In the second form it is established by means of the complete independence of the State from the Church, and of the Church from the State. In the third form, finally, this mutual independence and separation is defended and promoted, not as a theoretical principle of justice, but as that which in practice supplies the best *modus vivendi*. What should be our estimate of each of these forms, and what their proper and distinctive characteristics are, we must now consider in due order.

CHAPTER I

THESIS: *That the first form of liberalism is equivalent to materialism and atheism.*

THIS IS THE FORM OF ABSOLUTE LIBER-
alism about which the preceding article was concerned. It
conceives the State as the highest power to which human-
ity in its social progress can raise itself. Not only has the State nothing above it, but it has not even anything equal to it, or anything
that is not subject to it. It itself is the supreme and universal power
which nothing can resist and which everything must obey. It is the
norm *par excellence*; it is the regulator of all human relationships; in
whose view there is no right, either individual or domestic, which
is inviolable, and much less any sacred right of which any other
society might boast. For all rights are derived from it in virtue of
the social will, which, being first manifested by public opinion,
is then erected into a law by the representatives of the people in
parliaments. And because the social will is essentially progressive,
it follows that no law, no institution enjoys immutability, but all
are subject to an indefinite social progress. Always, however, the
law of the State, as long as it is and remains the law of the State,
exhibits the supreme rule of human behavior.

This theory, as anyone may see for himself, is that which more
or less rules the modern constitutions of Europe, resting on the
"Declaration of the Rights of Man." According to its principles, the
Church loses not only all preeminence in relation to the State, but
also even her status as a perfect and independent society. At most
she can only continue as a simple society, like any other association,

receiving its existence from the State. And, as the State, according to its pure good pleasure and to the degree that it judges expedient, allows her to enjoy a public existence, thus it defines what are the limits within which the rights which it concedes may be exercised, always reserving for itself fundamental authority. Thus, finally, it has come to such a pass that the present condition of the Church is worse from a certain standpoint than her condition under the pagan Emperors, when the intermittent violence of the bloody persecutions allowed her to breath freely occasionally.

Now, however, what we must think of the intrinsic character of this theory is easily seen. In the first place, it contains an implicit denial of the spirituality of the soul as well as of its immortality. For with what justification would it conceive the State as the supreme authority, if it did not restrict the destiny of man exclusively to the sphere of organic and material life? For whoever once admits that man's destiny is not complete in this world and that there remains for him after the present life another immortal life, is, willy-nilly, at once forced to admit that only a religious society can be supreme, that, namely, which guides man and aids him to advance to his supreme good. Nor is there any reason at all for anyone to think that the end of temporal prosperity, which is looked after by the State, is that supreme good to which all else must yield and be subordinated, unless he at the same time thinks of man as being evolved from pure matter and as returning to matter. Therefore, absolute liberalism is equivalent to materialism.

But the root-error whence all others spring is, properly speaking, the denial of God. For, certainly, if one supposes that there is no God, or (what comes to the same thing) that there is no God distinct from the world, it is easy to understand that man is the highest power in the universe, that is, man multiplied by association into a multitude and constituted as a civil community. Indeed, in such a man is the final limit of perfection to which unproduced matter has attained. He, in consequence, is his own absolute master; he the one who lays down standards for himself and his subordinates concerning that which he is pleased to call good or evil, just or unjust. But no greater absurdity is conceivable, once a personal God is recognized, the Creator of heaven and earth, who is above all things which are or can be imagined as distinct from him, and ineffably above them. For then, in that God, living and true, by inevitable necessity we must recognize the Supreme Lord and Law-giver of the universe, before whom man and society, and those who preside over society, must of necessity bow down. Then not the State, not public opinion, not the whims of progress, but the immutable principles of morality divinely imprinted upon our minds must be accepted as the supreme rule of human action in both the private and the public order. Then, finally, the highest human authorities will appear to have no right to govern other than a power which is subordinated to God's authority, so that it is only authorized to rule peoples in accordance with the will of that God, to whom all human authority is subject.

> Hear, therefore, ye kings, and understand: learn, ye that are judges of the ends of the earth. Give ear, you that rule the people, and that please yourselves in multitudes of nations: For power is given you by the Lord, and strength by the Most High, who will examine your works, and search out your thoughts: Because being ministers of his kingdom, you have not judged rightly, nor kept the law of justice, nor walked according to the will of God. Horribly and speedily will he appear to you: for a most severe judgment shall be for them that bear rule. For to him that is little, mercy is granted: but the mighty shall be mightily tormented. For God will not except any man's person, neither will he stand in awe of any man's greatness: for he made the little and the great, and he hath equally care of all. But a greater punishment

is ready for the more mighty. To you, therefore, O kings, are these my words, that you may learn wisdom, and not fall from it. (*Wisdom*, 6: 2–10.)

This is the conception of political power the divine Scriptures inculcate: surely quite a different one from the notion of a power that is the fount and origin of all right! Behold how in a political ruler they recognize no more than a servant: "For he is God's minister for good," says the apostle (Rom. 13:4). A minister, I repeat, applying the law which he has received, and from which, if he should deviate at all, not only is there no longer due him the obedience of his subjects, but the most severe punishment from God. All this is most evident from the standpoint of rigorous logic alone for everyone who acknowledges a God, and does not even admit the shadow of a doubt. Wherefore, that monstrous conception of the State, supreme law of public morality, having dominion over religious society itself, so that it concedes, takes away, limits or measures its rights in public law according to the necessity or utility of its own political purpose — such a conception, I say, agrees essentially with the absolute denial of God: that is, of the living and true God, who is something more than an empty idea invented for keeping the vile mob in bounds.

Nor does it make any difference to say that this conception still leaves religion free in the individual and private sphere. For this is nothing. First, since individuals are not any more self-sufficient for religious life than they are for temporal life, indeed much less so, religious society is for them a necessary means, so that they will be formed by divine discipline. And therefore, to claim for itself dominion over social religion, is, necessarily, to subordinate even one's individual and private religion. Secondly, because religion does not alter its nature when it passes from the public to the private order. If, therefore, in the public order it is reckoned among the merely human things which exist for a political end and are placed under the dominion of the State, likewise in the private order, by its very nature it takes its place as a mere human affair, for example, of an empty opinion concerning God, who, although in reality a sort of chimera, is still, nevertheless, thought to exist by superstitious and weak-minded men. Hence, in every way, from start to finish, absolute liberalism, that is, the kind which asserts the domination of the State over the Church, amounts to the same thing as pure and downright atheism. And since there seems to be no way of avoiding this conclusion, we need not belabor the point further, but we must now consider a milder form of liberalism, with which the following chapter is concerned.

CHAPTER II

THESIS: *That moderate Liberalism is reducible, if not to formal Atheism, certainly to Manichaeism.*[1]

T
HE LIBERALISM OF WHICH WE HAVE SPO-
ken up to now is so utterly at variance with the meaning of
its name, that you might think the name had been imposed
as a way of avoiding facing up to its real meaning, as the Furies
of ancient fable were given the title Eumenides or 'gracious god-
desses'. For in truth, that liberty from which it takes its name, if it
is the liberty of impiety, is yet much more the liberty of carefully
planned tyranny, of despotism worse than any barbarism. Hence
its extremism has displeased many who, in consequence. undertook
to construct (pardon the expression) a more liberal liberalism. And
this is the liberalism which is said to be moderate, and which, so
far as words go, no longer defends the absolute domination of the
State over the Church, but only the complete independence of
the former from the latter, and their entire separation from each
other, according to the celebrated formula: *A free Church in a free
State*. It professes not to deny the religious order, not even the
supernatural religious order, the absolute autonomy due to it, but
merely to desire that one should utterly ignore it when it comes
to ordering the affairs of political society. For religious affairs and
political affairs are two entirely different things. Each has a distinct

---

[1] Cf. Matteo Liberatore, *La Chiesa e lo Stato. cap. 1, art, 1, 3.*

† Liberatore (1810–1892) was an Italian Jesuit philosopher and theologian who
was part of the Thomistic revival and co-founded in 1850 the *Civiltà Cattolica*, a
Jesuit periodical known for its defense of the rights of the Church.

scope and purpose, and the methods of civil society are not those of religious society. And how may we mix up those matters which from the very nature of things are separate? For the rest, we must not depart from the general principle of justice, by which we are commanded to render to everyone his due, both to Caesar the things which are Caesar's, and to God the things which are God's: so that, in a word, ecclesiastical society shall enjoy its own rights and likewise civil society, and, since there is room for both beneath the sun, let each go its own way, not bothering at all about the affairs of the other.

You may hear the moderate liberal speaking thus:

> No more union between Church and State. Since the Church has no more in common with governments than governments have in common with religion, why let them meddle in each other's affairs! The individual professes after his own fashion the form of worship which he chooses according to his taste; as a member of the State, however, he has no particular form of worship. The State recognizes all religions, assures them all equal protection, guarantees them equal liberty, such is the regime of tolerance; and it behooves us to pronounce it good, excellent, and salutary, to maintain it at all costs, and to spread it unceasingly. One can say that this regime is of divine right. God himself has established it in creating man free; he puts it into practice by making his sun to shine alike upon the just and the unjust. Regarding those who disregard the truth, God will have his day of justice, which man does not have the right to hasten. Each Church, as being free in a free State, will incorporate its converts, direct its faithful, and excommunicate its dissidents; the State will take no account of these things, will excommunicate no one,

and will never be excommunicated. The civil law will
recognize no ecclesiastical immunity, no religious prohibition, no religious obligation; the temple will pay
the tax on doors and windows, theological students will
do military service, the bishops will serve on juries or
in the national guard, the priest may marry, if he will,
be divorced, if he will, and be remarried, if he will. On
the other hand, there will be no more civil disabilities or
prohibitions than there will be immunities of another
kind. Every religion will preach, publish, hold proces-
sions, ring its bells, anathematize and bury according to
its fancy, and the ministers of religion will be all that a
citizen can be. Nothing, so far as the State is concerned,
will prevent a bishop from commanding his company in
the national guard, keeping shop, or conducting a business; and no more shall anything prevent his Church,
or the Council, or the Pope, from being able to depose
him. The State does not take cognizance of anything
but the facts of public order.[2]

This is certainly more plausible, indeed, to many it will seem
so thoroughly in keeping with the rule of equity, that nothing
could be more so. Except that, if one considers the matter a little
more attentively, he will easily see that the position is untenable
by reason of the irreducible dualism which it introduces. And this,
indeed, Boniface VIII had long ago remarked in the bull *Unam
Sanctam*, where he says that the defender of the absolute independence whether of the Church from the State or of the State from
the Church, resists the ordinance of God, *unless he imagines like
Manichaeus that there are two first principles, which we declare to*

[2] Louis Veuillot, *L'illusion libérale*, § I.

† Veuillot (1813–1883) was a journalist whose works — especially in the periodical, *L'Univers*, — defended the Papacy and the importance of a Catholic social order.

be false and heretical. And truly it is the case, because the doctrine
logically agrees with the absurd beliefs of the Manichaeans, or certainly with what is equivalent to them, whether the Manichaeans
are understood according to their belief that there were two gods as
well as two natures in each and every principle, or according to their
assertion that there were also two souls in every man, "one from
God and sharing his nature, the other from the face of darkness
which God neither begat, nor produced, nor put forth, nor cast off,
but which has its own life, its own place, its own offspring and life,
in short, its own kingdom and unbegotten origin."[3]

And in the first place, it is certainly self-evident, that if the principle of the whole world is one, or as it is said in Ecclesiasticus
(*Sirach*), I, 8, *There is one most high almighty Creator*, there also
will be one order of the universe, one supreme end of creation.
And it is also evident that this end, most sublime on account of
him who orders it, and most beneficial for those who are ordered,
can be none other than the glory of God and the eternal happiness
of the rational creature, for whose sake all lesser things were made.
Finally, it is evident that to this end every inferior end should be
subordinated, provided it is true that secondary goods have the
status of means with respect to the primary end, and that means are
necessarily subordinate to the end. Hence, with irresistible clarity
the conclusion arises: that the political State itself is subordinated
to that one and unique supreme end, from which it is no more
permitted to depart than, for example, a carpenter may depart from
the purpose of the architect for whom it is his duty to prepare the
lumber and arrange it for use in erecting a house. I say, however,
the consequence of an irresistible clarity, because there is no way
of evading it, except by denying the major premise from which it
flows. Whoever, therefore, maintains that the purpose of the State
and the purpose of religion are entirely disconnected from each

---

[3] Augustine, *De Vera Religione*, c. 9; cf., also *De Moribus Ecclesiæ*, Lib. I, c. 10.

other, and because of this are completely disconnected or separate powers, each of which governs its own affairs: on account of that he implicitly denies the unity of the first principle, he says there is one creator of spiritual things, another of temporal; one god by whom man is ordered to civil life and another by whom he is ordered to religious life. Like Manichaeus, therefore, he imagines that there are two principles, and, if perchance he differs in anything from Manichaeus, it is only in this, that his attitude is still worse. For, the author of temporal things, whom Manichaeus considered an evil god, he will without difficulty regard as the god of light and progress, that other god, the creator of spiritual things, whom Manichaeus called the good god, he will call a god of darkness and obscurantism. Indeed, it is customary with those who are wont to make historical arguments against history, philosophical arguments against philosophy, and scriptural arguments against the Scriptures: it is customary, I say, to appeal to that passage in the Gospels where we are bidden to render to Caesar the things that are Caesar's and to God the things that are God's. Now, concerning the true ground for distinguishing the things which are Caesar's from the things which are God's, there is no place for discussion here. Meanwhile, however, it may be permissible to ask this one thing: whether, or not, Caesar is to be regarded as a creature of God. If as a creature of God, how, I ask, is he independent of God, having the right of disposing his own affairs without any regard to God, to the law of God, and to the religion which God has instituted? If, however, not a creature of God, then, by your own confession, it is asserted there is one god of temporal matters opposed to the creator of spiritual things, and so, following Manichaeus, they imagine there are two principles.

And not only two first principles, but it will also be necessary to posit two souls in each single man, and with far greater reason for reverting to this new dualism than the Manichaeans had. The Manichaeans, indeed, since they were conscious of two wills in deciding, concluded that there were two natures of two different minds, one good, the other evil. Nevertheless, they did not conceive of them as traveling their different ways simultaneously, but as struggling against each other, so that, when one prevailed, the other was forced to cease from activity: which was not so absolutely opposed to the possible reduction into one soul, turning alternately now to good, now to evil, until by the victory of one tendency over the other, the whole will as one should begin to be confirmed in one alternative only, which formerly had been partially divided. Now, however, moderate liberalism, by separating the civil order from the religious order, separates the citizen from the Christian, the philosopher from the believer, the public from the private man, the politician from the member of the Church. It separates, I say, not as belligerents are separated, one of whom wishes to suppress the other, but as independent beings are separated, each one of whom pursues his own way, and regularly discharges at the same time with the other his own duty, regardless of how much both are moved by separate authorities, to disparate and contrary objectives. And this, I say, is absolutely and essentially incompatible with any reduction to unity, nor is it otherwise conceivable than by positing in one and the same man two souls, two minds, two consciences really distinct from each other: the one atheistic, the other religious; the one believing, the other unbelieving; the one intent on temporal things without regard or respect to spiritual things, the other intent on spiritual things and, as it were, placed in a heavenly realm outside this world; one by whom he serves Caesar, and the other by whom he serves God.

> No wealth of eloquence can hide for long the depth of incurable misery, no words in any language have the elasticity to harmonize and hold together such contradictions: Free cooperation, reciprocal independence of two powers, etc. What do these high-sounding phrases

signify? What results practically from the free cooper-
ation of soul and body, the reciprocal independence of
matter and spirit?[4]

Whatever way, therefore, the problem is viewed, that mutual
independence of the two powers, or the fiction of a free Church
in a free State, restores a new Manichaeism, theoretically indeed
absurd, in practice impossible. For how will you conceive of two
forces acting regularly on the same changeable entity, unless there
is subordination between them, through which the contrariety of
impulses is eliminated, and the necessary unity of direction preserved? Which not even the moderate liberalists themselves attempt
to conceal whenever they descend from the abstract rhetoric of
words to the field of concrete reality. The necessary subordination
of either the State to the Church, or of the Church to the State,
does not escape them. But the first would be outrageous; for that
would be to renounce the first and most essential principle of
liberalism. Hence, compelled by necessity, and not being able to
maintain themselves in the apparent equilibrium of reciprocal independence, they fall into absolute liberalism, and place the Church
under the hand and power of the State, as often as, in the judgment
of the State itself, reasons of state and temporal interest would
seem to demand it.

> It is necessary that there should be one superior power
> which has the right to remove all doubts and solve all
> difficulties. This power is that to whom it is given to
> weigh all interests, that on which the public and general
> order depends, to whom alone it belongs to assume the
> name of power in the proper sense.... Religious soci-
> ety has had to recognize in civil society, more ancient,

4 Veuillot, *L'illusion libérale*, § 24.

more powerful, and of which it becomes a partner, the
authority necessary to assure the union, and the suprem-
acy which makes the interest of the State prevail in all
points of discipline wherever their affairs are mixed.[5]

One would have to admit two powers absolutely
equal, whose concurrence would produce a sort of political Manichaeism, and would result in perilous conflicts
with a refusal to compromise.[6]

And thus there happens to them what usually happens to those
who, while holding fast to the root of the error, seek how they may
obtain for the error a better appearance. They not only do not suc-
ceed, but, becoming lame on both sides, fall with ungraceful awk-
wardness into the ditch they desired to avoid. But it is this selfsame
deformity of lameness which will appear even more conspicuously
in the third form of liberalism of which it now remains to speak.

---

[5] Jean-Étienne-Marie Portalis, *Discours et travaux inédits sur le Code Civil.*

† Portalis (1746–1807) was a French politician and jurist during the French
Revolution and the First Empire.

[6] Dupin, *Rapport sur les travaux inédits de Portalis.*

CHAPTER III

THESIS: *That the so-called Liberalism of "liberal Catholics" defies classification, and has one distinctive and characteristic trait, namely, that of complete and absolute incoherence.*

THE TRUTH OF THIS ASSERTION CAN BE shown even from the mere examination of the terms which are joined together in that phrase: liberal Catholic.

For a Catholic is one who professes what the Christian faith teaches, and above all, that which it hands on as a foundation for this in its catechism: that man is created to praise, reverence, and serve God, after the manner that accords with the good-pleasure of his divine will, and thus in the end to save his own soul. And he also professes that the other things placed on the face of the earth are created for the sake of man, so that they may help him in pursuing the end for which he is created; on account of which, consequently, it follows that man is to use them or abstain from them as much as they help him or hinder him in pursuing his end; especially since, by the testimony of Truth himself, it profits a man nothing if he gain the whole world, but suffer the loss of his own soul, indeed that it profits him exceedingly to enter maimed or lamed or with only one eye into life everlasting, rather than having two hands and two feet and two eyes to go into Gehenna, into unquenchable fire, where the worm dies not and the fire is not extinguished. Hence prosperity in the present life which is obtained at the cost of our soul's salvation, is false, pernicious, deadly, and in the highest degree detestable; and this present life itself must be wholly and entirely regulated with a view to the future life; all temporal things must be

subordinated to eternal things, and therefore the direction of the
power which presides over temporal things should be subordinate
to the direction of the higher power, to which the procuring of our
eternal end is believed to have been committed by God himself,
together with the promise of perpetual divine assistance. Is not all
this involved in the principles of every Catholic, if only he does not
utterly give the lie to his own profession of faith?

Take now the profession of the liberal. Certainly a liberal, as
we now speak of liberals, is one who professes and eulogizes and
approves of and promotes the so-called immortal principles of the
year 1789. We must, therefore, see what these principles contain.
Now these principles — setting aside once for all that which is not
unique to them but has been received from the ancient and common treasury of natural justice and equity, about which there is
no controversy — when reduced to the minimum and construed
in the best way possible, proclaim the independence of human
from divine things, the withdrawal of the civil order from religious law, the divorce of the regime of temporal things from the
regime which aims at the ultimate and supreme end; finally, in a
word, the removal of the orbit of the State into a separate sphere
in which the dominion of God ceases, the obligation of acknowl-
edging and worshipping him ceases, the ordering of man to everlasting life ceases, and only the eye which regards the present life is
opened, while the eye which is to show him the way to the future
life remains closed.

> Nothing is more laborious and fruitless than an excur-
> sion into the research of the principles of '89. One
> encounters there an abundance of empty verbiage, of
> banalities and meaningless phrases. M. Cousin, who has
> undertaken the task of shedding light on those mysteries
> which bear the redoubtable and glorious name of the
> principles of the French Revolution, reduces them to

three: *the sovereignty of the nation; the emancipation of the individual, or justice; the progressive diminution of ignorance, misery, and vice, or civil charity.* Tocqueville does not contradict M. Cousin; he only demonstrates without difficulty that '89 discovered nothing good and acceptable that is peculiar to the banner of '89. All were strongly rooted in the ancient French constitution, and its development would have been more general and solid if the Revolution had never put its hand or rather its knife to the task. Before '89, France believed itself to be quite free, and, long before, one had glimmers of equality before the law, following from the long-established practice of equality before God. Charity manifested itself by the rather large number of charitable institutions and congregations; public education was more liberal, more solid, and more widespread than at the present day. . . . If, then, the principles of '89 are what M. Cousin says they are, how does the Catholic faith contradict them? Liberal Catholics and non-liberal Catholics alike have not only respected them, but have practiced and defended them.[1]

This is what is contained in the immortal principles of 1789, and that according to the most benign interpretation of which they admit; for, in the understanding of the Fathers of the Revolution, which by the way is alone consistent with the logic of things, they import involve? absolute and complete secularization, that is, the banishment of the theocratic principle from the world, and the definitive rupture of the whole of human of society with the Church, with Jesus Christ, with God, indeed with the idea of God and of the last vestige of him.

[1] Veuillot, *L'Ilusion Libérale,* § 32.

But it is time to expose the arcana of '89, and to ascertain the point at which the liberal Catholic faith will have to stop being liberal or stop being Catholic. There exists *one* principle of '89 which is the Revolutionary principle *par excellence*, and for it alone the whole Revolution and all its principles came into existence. One is not a revolutionary until the moment that he avows it, one does not cease to be a revolutionary until the moment he abjures it. Either way, everything follows from this; it is the one supremely significant issue; it raises between revolutionaries and Catholics a wall of separation across which liberal Catholic Pyramuses and the revolutionary Thisbes will never make anything pass but their fruitless sighs. This unique principle of '89 is that which the revolutionary politeness of the conservatives of 1830 calls the secularization of society; it is that which the revolutionary frankness of the age, the Solidaires and M. Quinet brutally calls the expulsion of the theocratic principle; it is the rupture with the Church, with Jesus Christ, with God, with all acknowledgement, with all presence and all appearance of the idea of God, in human society.[2]

In any case, and accepting for the time being the mitigated interpretation, who is there that does not see in them such an irreducibility to the fundamental principles of Christianity, that every attempt at reconciliation must necessarily end in complete incoherence? Moreover, this *a priori* estimate is entirely confirmed, if the arguments of liberal Catholics are weighed, one after another.

Incoherence appears immediately when they distinguish between abstract principles and their application, admitting that,

---

[2] Veuillot, *op. cit.*, § 33.

speculatively speaking, those things are indeed true which we say concerning the necessary union and subordination of powers, and that they, again speculatively speaking, by no means dissent from this; but that the object of speculation is one thing, what holds true in the concrete order of things, however, something else, where there are many things entirely at variance with theoretical conditions. And so they imagine that they have satisfied truth by relegating it to the regions of the abstract. But, with all due respect to them, those principles which they call abstract, do they or do they not pertain to moral matters, that is, do they or do they prescribe the norm of human acts and the rule of right conduct; conduct, which in human society is rightly directed so as to achieve its purpose? And if they are wholly practical dictates, as is self-evident, how is it not the height of incoherence for anyone to accept them and at the same time to be unwilling to apply them? For from the fact that the concrete order of things differs from the ideal conditions of theory, this alone follows: that it will never happen that in real life they will be realized with that perfection which pure speculation exhibits. But, indeed, with the same sort of argument I could prove that the precepts of virtue should be left in the realm of speculation, because the human condition does not admit of such a high standard of rectitude. With the same sort of argument, likewise, I might demonstrate that mathematics can or should have no application to the arts, because the ideally exact triangle of geometry has no existence in the concrete, or because the experimental effect is always at variance with the rigor of calculus.

Again, there is incoherence in the distinction which they make between that which *de jure* is fitting or due to the Church, and that which *de facto* is useful to the Church, saying: that as a matter of fact, the regime of union has always been pernicious to the Church; that the Church, as a matter of fact, has never endured greater harm than it did from those pretend bishops, guardian princes, as the interminable quarrels with the Byzantine emperors, the Germanic

Kaisers, and the Kings of France, England, Spain, etc., attest; that the Church, alas! is perishing on account of the temporal props with which she has inadvisedly equipped herself; and that therefore there remains one saving remedy, one haven of refuge, liberty! Liberty is what shall restore the lost crown to the majestic brow of the Church; liberty must be relied as on a faithful friend, nor must she ever abandon liberty on account of *a priori* principles, which must be left, with all due reverence, of course, safe and sound in their ideal sphere.

> The Church is perishing on account of the unwarranted support she has willed for herself. The time has come for her to change her attitude; her children must make her aware of the advisability of this. She must renounce all her coercive power over consciences that she denies to governments. No more alliance between the Church and the State.... Our liberal Catholic waxed enthusiastic in unfolding these marvels. He maintained that no exception could be taken to his position; that he was a spokesman for reason, faith, and the spirit of the times. As regards the spirit of the times, no one contested his assertion. As regards reason and faith, however, they did not fail to put forward objections, but he shrugged his shoulders and was never at a loss for an answer. It is true that outrageous assertions and outrageous contradictions cost him no qualms. He always started off on the same foot, protesting that he is a Catholic, a child of the Church, an obedient child; but also a man of his times, a member of a human race grown old and mature, of an age to govern itself. To the arguments drawn from history he answered that mankind in its present stage of maturity is a new world, in the presence of which history no longer proves anything. But this does not prevent

him from exploiting the historical argument whenever
he finds it opportune. To the words of the Fathers of the
Church, he sometimes opposed other words of theirs,
sometimes he said that the Fathers spoke for their times,
but that we must think and act according to our times.
Confronted with the texts of Scripture, he had the same
resourcefulness. Either he threw out some seemingly
contrary texts, or he manufactured a gloss to support his
own interpretation, or finally he would say that this text
was fine for the Jews and for their particular little state.
Nor is he to any greater degree embarrassed by dogmatic
bulls of the *Roman Curia*.... They are, says he, disci-
plinary formulas laid down for those times, but which
have no *raison d'être* today. The French Revolution has
buried these rules along with that world on which they
weighed so heavily. Constraint has been abolished; the
man of today is capable of liberty and wants no other
law! This regime, which arouses such fear in you, he
continues in sibylline tones, is for all that the very one
which will save the Church, and the only one which
can save her. For the rest, the human race is making a
stand to impose this order, it will indeed be necessary
to submit, and that has already been done. See whether
anyone would be able to oppose anything whatsoever
to this triumphant force, if indeed any one had even
wanted to do so, if indeed anyone, with the exception of
yourselves, ever dreamt of doing so. Intolerant Catholics,
you were more absolute than God the Father, who created man for liberty; more Christian than God the Son,
who desired to establish his law for no other purpose
than for liberty. Here you are, more Catholic than the
Pope, because the Pope, in approving them, consecrates
modern constitutions, which are all inspired and replete

with the spirit of liberty. I say that the Pope, the Vicar of Jesus Christ, approves of these constitutions, because he permits you to take the oath of allegiance to them, to obey them and to defend them. Now freedom of religion is contained in them, also the atheism, of the state. It is necessary to put up with that, and without doubt you do put up with that. Why then fight against it? Your resistance is vain; your regrets are not only foolish, but disastrous as well. They cause the Church to be hated, and they hinder the work of us who are liberals, your saviors, in that they cause our sincerity to be suspected. Instead, then, of drawing down upon yourselves certain and probably terrible defeat, run to the arms of liberty, salute her, embrace her, love her. She will be to you a good and faithful friend, and she will give you more than you can ever repay. Faith stagnates under the yoke of the authority which protects her. Obliged to defend herself, she will rise again; the ardor of polemics will restore her to life. What will not the Church undertake when she will be able to undertake everything? How can she fail to touch the hearts of peoples, when they see her abandoned by the powerful ones of the world, living solely by her own genius and her own virtues? In the midst of the confusion of doctrines and the corruption of morals, she alone will appear as pure and intent only on goodness. She will be the last refuge, the impregnable rampart of morality, the family, religion, and liberty! Everything has its limits, and so even the breath of our orator gives out at last. . . .

The liberal has recovered his breath. As soon as he has recovered it, he resumes his discourse, and it is quite evident that what he had just heard made no impression on him whatsoever, if indeed he had heard it at all.

He added any number of words to those which he had
already spoken in great profusion, but said nothing new.
It was all a most intricate medley of historical arguments
against history, of biblical arguments against the Bible,
of patristic arguments against history, the Bible and the
Fathers, and against common sense. . . . He brought up
again the modern world, emancipated humanity, the
Church asleep and on the verge of awakening to rejuve-
nate her creed. The dead past, the radiant future, liberty,
love, democracy, humanity, are interspersed throughout
like the false diamonds which the ladies now-a-days scat-
ter through their false tresses. All this appeared neither
more clear nor more true than the first time he said it.
He became conscious of this and he told us that we
were separating ourselves from the world and from the
living Church, which would be well rid of us. He almost
cursed us, and finally left us filled with consternation
at his folly.[3]

Thus they argue, but incoherently. *First*, because, if *a priori* the
principles express an order instituted and intended by God, it is
impossible that their neglect should result in greater utility to the
Church. *Second*, because the facts which are adduced prove that
man through his own perversity often corrupts the institutions
of God, but they do not prove that the divine order ought for
this reason to be repudiated or set aside. *Third*, because the historical argument is faulty on account of incomplete enumeration,
referring only to the evils which happened under the regime of
union, and concealing and omitting the immense benefits that
abounded, so that it is clear that, though the protection of mon-
archs, even if it sometimes degenerated into oppression, for the

[3] Veuillot, *L'illusion libérale,* § 1–4.

most part nevertheless was a safeguard and powerful aid to the Church. *Fourth*, because the fault of an incomplete enumeration is aggravated by the lack of comparison with the evils which spring necessarily from the separation of Church and State, and which, as present-day experience is witness, are vastly greater. *Fifth*, because nothing stands out more as an example of a disconnected and incoherent argumentation than its ultimate conclusion of the necessity of having recourse to liberty. Liberty, indeed, inclined towards evil, prone towards irreligion, is the actual cause of all the evil, and it is precisely this very liberty which is held up as a remedy therefore!

But, they say, such a union and subordination of the two powers, however desirable in itself, now at least is impossible; for the spirit of modernity is opposed to it, against which it is useless to struggle. Prudence, therefore, counsels the acceptance of the new state of affairs, whether for the purpose of preventing things from becoming constantly worse, or of getting the best results possible under existing conditions. And this is the plea on which, when other arguments fail, they finally take their stand. Except that, by saying this, as Liberatore rightly remarks, they fall into a worse incoherence than before, in that they deviate entirely from the question at issue. For the dispute between us is not whether, presupposing the defiant attitude of the world, it would not be well to bear patiently that which we have no power over, and in the meantime to give ourselves wholeheartedly to the task of avoiding greater evils and of bringing forth the good which remains possible. Rather the question is whether it is right to *approve* this social condition which liberalism introduces, to praise the principles which are fundamental to this order of things, and to promote them by word, teaching, and deed, as those do who along with the name Catholic claim for themselves the name of liberals. And they themselves especially are the ones who will never accomplish any good at all, because they are lame in both feet, and, attempting in vain a compromise, are neither recognized as genuine by the children of God, nor received as sincere by the children of the Revolution. They come, indeed, to the camp of the latter with the password of the principles of '89, but, because they pronounce the password badly, they are denied entrance.

In the Book of Judges (12:5–6) one reads that when the Galaadites, fighting against the Ephraimites, had overcome them, they conspired that not one of the fleeing Ephraimites might get away.

> And the Galaadites secured the fords of the Jordan. And when one of the number of Ephraim came thither in flight, and said: I beseech you let me pass: the Galaadites said to him: Art thou not an Ephraimite? If he said: I am not: they asked him: Say then, *Shibboleth*, which is interpreted, an ear of corn. But he answered: *Sibboleth*, not being able to express an ear of corn by the same letter. Then presently they took him and killed him in the very passage of the Jordan.

And thus too, it happens at the entrance to the gate of the camp of liberalism. To those who desire to enter it is said: Say then, *'Shibboleth*, which is interpreted the *secularization of society*. It makes a different, however, whether they pronounce it well or badly. Indeed liberal Catholics suffer in this from a defect of the tongue, and they are unable to enunciate the sacramental word as is proper. Therefore they are not admitted, and they have merit neither with men nor with God, because they exhibit in themselves that dualism of which Scripture speaks: "One building up and one pulling down, what profit hath he but labor? One praying and one cursing, whose voice will God hear?" (*Ecclesiasticus*, 34:28–29.)

> They willingly swear by the principles of '89; they call them the *immortal* principles. It is the *Shibboleth* which gives entrance to the camp of mighty liberalism. But

there is a manner of pronouncing it, and our Catholics cannot quite manage it. . . . This is why they pronounce the *Shibboleth* badly, and why the Revolution will not open to them. The Revolution is more fair to them than they are to themselves. It detects their Catholicity, and it does them the honor of not believing them when they try to convince it that they are no more Catholics than persons outside the Church, that nothing will come of their Catholicity, and that they will play their atheistic part very well in that ideal form of government without religion and without God.[4]

---

[4] Veuillot, *op. cit.,* § 32–34.

AFTERWORD

LREADY THE PRESAGE OF A BETTER state of things has made its appearance, in as much as those who are today preeminent in the political and economic sciences, from day to day more and more recognize, and without hesitation acknowledge, how disastrous was the work of the Revolution, and how deadly are the fruits of liberty, of *liberal* or rather libertine liberty, , of the liberty of the social contract, the liberty of the ideologues of 1789. These indeed, did not hesitate to proclaim that the only cause of public evils and the corruption of governments was ignorance or contempt of the rights of man, of which the first, they said, is liberty, with the necessary complement of equality and fraternity.

> The representatives of the people, as constituted in the National Assembly, considering that ignorance, neglect or contempt of the rights of man are the sole causes of public misfortunes and the corruption of governments, have resolved to set forth in a solemn declaration the natural, inalienable, and sacred rights of man.... Article I. — Men are born and remain free and equal in rights, etc., etc.[1]

O levity! O foolishness! O folly! And surely, their liberty has ended in a despotism worse than any barbarism, of the powerful over the weak; their equality in an ever-increasing multitude of proletarians on the one side, and an oligarchy of always more powerful millionaires on the other; their fraternity, finally, in sowing

---

[1] *Déclaration des droits de l'homme de 1789*

everywhere the seeds of internal division, and of implacable hatred of class against class. Nor have these things escaped the notice of certain select thinkers of our own times.

> What is the meaning in economic life of the freedom of labor, the freedom of trade, the freedom of ownership, if it be not a facility for the unleashing of all cupidity aimed at exploiting all weakness, or, according to the expression of one publicist, the freedom that one enjoys in the forest? And what have we gained by all these beautiful theories? Never have souls been more anxious, never have the people been more discontented, never have conditions been more precarious. Is this the political liberty which we won? Half of the citizens are quite opposed to all that is claimed as a right by the other half. Is this equality? Never have we had so many proletarians, and, likewise, never so many bloated millionaires. Is this fraternity? Never has there been so much selfishness, never so many factions, never so much fermentation of social strife, etc.[2]

True, there are many who still remain on the surface of the problem, not perceiving as yet the essential character of the Revolution, which is satanic. But there are others who search more deeply into the matter, and correctly understand *that the religious question underlies all others that are now being agitated*; that the plague of political and economic liberalism was born of the atheistic and antichristian liberalism of which we have spoken above; finally, that the social order can in no way be upheld and stabilized, unless the Church resumes the direction of social affairs. It is to be hoped, therefore, that with the assistance of divine grace, these seeds

---

[2] La Tour du Pin, *Vers un ordre social chrétien*, 3, § I.

may come to maturity, that these principles which are theoretically acknowledged may become the foundations of a restoration. And such a restoration we call for with our whole heart, knowing that under the pagan legislation, under which we now live, individual Christians can exist, indeed, but a truly Christian society cannot. In this, then, we seek wholly the kingdom of God and his justice, although we do not reject those other things which are added to that, nor are we unaware with regard to the beneficial influence of the Church what has been written: that she is useful for all things, and she has the promise of the life that now is, and of that which is to come. (cf. I Tim. 4:8.)

ABOUT THE TRANSLATORS

MSGR. GEORGE BARRY O'TOOLE, (1886–1944) was born in Toledo, Ohio. He was ordained in 1911 and is known for his involvement in the founding of the Catholic University of Beijing, becoming its first president (1925–1927). He later taught theology and philosophy at St. Vincent's Seminary in Latrobe, Pennsylvania and was the head of the philosophy department at Duquesne University in Pittsburgh. He was involved in founding a Catholic Worker house in Pittsburgh, and the Catholic Radical Alliance, an organization supporting labor's right to organize, inspired by the encyclical, *Rerum Novarum*. In connection with the latter Msgr. O'Toole actively supported the Heinz strike in 1937. In 1940 he testified to the United State Senate against the Selective Service Act of 1940. Among his other interests was animal biology which he taught as a professor at Seton Hill College. He wrote a four-hundred page book, *The Case Against Evolution*, in 1925.

THOMAS STORCK writes on a wide variety of topics pertaining to Catholic social teaching and Catholic culture and history. He is the author of five books, *The Catholic Milieu* (1987), *Foundations of a Catholic Political Order* (1998), *Christendom and the West* (2000), *From Christendom to Americanism and Beyond* (Angelico Press, 2015), and *An Economics of Justice & Charity* (Angelico Press, 2017). He is a contributing editor of *The Distributist Review* and a member of the editorial board of *The Chesterton Review*. Many of his essays and articles may be found on the website: www.thomasstorck.org.

AROUCA PRESS
REPRINTS

Dogmatic Theology (Msgr. Van. Noort)

Volume 1: The True Religion
Volume 2: Christ's Church
Volume 3: The Sources of Revelation, Divine Faith

CPSIA information can be obtained
at www.ICGtesting.com
Printed in the USA
FSHW012153221219
65374FS